MARRIAGE:

A
DISCOVERY
TOGETHER

MARRIAGE:

A
DISCOVERY
TOGETHER

John G. Quesnell

Notre Dame, Indiana 46556

Quesnell, John G 1936-
   Marriage: a discovery together.

   Includes bibliographies.
   1. Marriage.   2. Interpersonal relations.
I. Title.
HQ728.Q47   301.42   73-18020
ISBN 0-8190-0484-7

1773-7783-8793M

To My Parents

Foreword

The title of this book, *Marriage: A Discovery Together,* establishes the tone for the discussion that is to follow. Throughout the book, one becomes dramatically aware of the potential of the marital relationship. The author demonstrates that through marriage, one becomes more aware of oneself, his relationship with significant others, and his relationship with God. Within marriage, one can perhaps discover a good deal about the intricate workings of one's mate and, in living together as a team, the marital pair might contribute positively to the larger community and even, hopefully, to their own children.

If anything is to be discovered in marriage, it is oneself. In no other interpersonal experience is there the opportunity to see ourselves so completely. Our finer qualities are reflected and amplified, while our less noble personality characteristics are painfully pointed out by the failure to respond honestly to the needs of one's spouse. The various refusals to take advantage of the opportunity to reveal and discover ourselves are given careful examination in the pages to follow. The focus of this book is not so much that a faulty marital interaction leads to individual problems, but that unresolved conflicts of the individual find expression in the disruption of marriage thereby further inhibiting personal growth. The author has pointed out that problems in communication result more from a failure to come effectively to grips with ourselves than they do from being unaware of various communication techniques.

Needless to say, the intact marriage can also profit from the insights of the author's experience. The book is intended for couples who are seeking to come to grips with disturbing intra and interpersonal problems as well as those who are seeking to add new dimension to their life together.

In reading this book, one realizes that marriage is a state of mind. As such, it transcends the societal features—legal, cultural, and religious—as an uniquely interpersonal relationship. The cultural controls are unquestionably important in preserving, sustaining, and perpetuating the family unit. They are, however, equally certainly, of no value in doing so if the interpersonal commitment is only legal or religious in nature. A cognitive and emotional union results in an extension of self, allowing completion of one's unfulfilled energies, while commitment only to the institution of marriage and not to the person usually succeeds in stifling individual energies and prohibiting personal growth. The result being disintegration of self and of the marriage subsequently.

Contrary to the opinion of many popular authors, Mr. Quesnell demonstrates that marriage need not be a stifling and dehumanizing experience. It is really up to the individual spouses to determine whether or not their marriage will be stifling or if they will take advantage of the opportunity it provides for a deep personal growth experience.

From a therapeutic point of view, this volume offers challenges not only to marriage partners, but to the person engaged in treating persons laboring under the burden of marriage problems. The formation of the psychological bond intrinsic to the marriage contract as well as the milestones of personal growth are carefully and clearly explained. The author's experience in treating marital interaction problems can be a useful resource to psychotherapists and pastoral counselors. Of particular interest is the frequently overlooked marital dysfunction of middle-aged or elderly couples. Overlooked, probably, because the violent interaction of younger, more recently married couples clamors for more attention while the inertia of years of not-growing and not-discovering seemingly presents little need for intervention. If marriage is a growth experience, it is so not just during the first years, but throughout its life span.

Hopefully, we will see more from Mr. Quesnell's experience in this straight-forward style. The present work reflects considerable skill in understanding the dynamics of family life.

John W. Haas, M.D.

Acknowledgments

I am deeply indebted to all of those who have influenced me during the past several years and who have played a role in the development of the ideas conveyed in this book. My patients and the participants in seminars and workshops I have conducted are the basic contributors to the ideas developed in the foregoing pages. I am also indebted to my many colleagues and friends who have encouraged me throughout these years.

Reverend Paul Marx, O.S.B. has been a professor, mentor, and colleague whose influence can be readily detected in the concepts that will be discussed.

I am very indebted to the staff in our office who have been so helpful and encouraging during the months that the manuscript was being prepared. I am especially indebted to Linda Hanson who patiently typed the several drafts of the manuscript.

I am grateful to Bishop John R. Roach, Reverends Mark Dosh, Earl Simonson, Richard Villano, and Ray Spack, Bill and Joan Cossette, and John and Sheila Kippley who so very kindly read and critiqued portions of the manuscript. Mrs. Jerry Jungquist assumed the tedious responsibility of proof-reading the final draft.

I am deeply indebted to Dr. John and Janet Haas who assumed the primary responsibility for reading and critiquing the preliminary manuscript drafts. The time they committed to this project along with their sense of enthusiasm and their encouragement far exceeded what one could expect of friends and colleagues. They made several suggestions which helped to clarify many of the concepts discussed in the following chapters.

Finally, I am very grateful to my wife Alice and to my children, Cathy, Mike, and Tim who all helped in some way during the months that the book was being written. Their greatest contribution, of course, was the love and encouragement they shared with me.

Contents

Section IV

DISCOVERING INTIMACY

Section V

WILL MARRIAGE SURVIVE?

Section I

THE DISCOVERY OF MARRIAGE

CHAPTER 1

I'm Going To Get Married
And Settle Down

When I was a twelve year old paper boy, I became acquainted with a middle-age couple who had been hospitalized after a serious automobile accident. Other than delivering papers to their respective rooms, I also ran errands for them and delivered messages between them. The hospital staff was concerned because their spirits were low and their recovery was not progressing as expected. Once after visiting with each of them, I commented to the nurse that it would sure be nice if they could be in the same room.

When I returned the next day, I was surprised to find them in the same room. The improvement in their spirits and physical condition was remarkable. As an impressionable pre-adolescent, it was reassuring to me to sense the love, warmth, and peace which permeated their relationship. Now some twenty-five years later, I find myself thinking of this couple. What made it possible for them to develop such a deep and meaningful relationship? Why is it that many couples are frustrated in their efforts to truly touch the soul of each other? What makes it possible to truly discover each other in marriage and to experience the joy that comes with such discovery? In the following pages, we will find how we can truly discover fulfillment in marriage.

There are certain mental attitudes which interfere with the discovery of marriage. For instance, the common theme of many fairy tales is that of a man and woman overcoming seemingly insurmountable obstacles to marriage such as differences in social background, parental objections, family feuds, etc. They eventually marry and "live happily ever after." These tales have given rise to popular romantic love myths such as "opposites attract," "there is only one person in the world who is meant for me," and "love will strike like lightning."

Other than believing they will achieve temporal ecstasy, couples also marry explaining, "We're going to get married and have a family," "We're going to get married and settle down," and "We're going to marry and live happily ever after." Rather than to get married and *settle down,* couples marry and *settle in.* They *settle in* to the old age or senescence of marriage. Because they have been conditioned to believe they were drawn together by celestial forces, they also believe their love will take care of itself. Couples fail to look at marriage as a vocation and a daily task. They believe their love is undying and will take care of itself. As a result of this thinking, husbands and wives fail to work at being married and become sloppy and careless about their life together.

Peggy says to herself, "Well, I'm just going to be home with Tom tonight, so I guess I'll set my hair." Peg then runs around the house in a pair of raggedy jeans, an old sweatshirt, and her hair wrapped up as though she were wired for sound. Tom, who has already gained twenty pounds during his first year of marriage, says to himself, "Well, I'm just going to be home with Peg tonight so I guess I will relax." Relaxation means he will sit around the house in his shorts and T-shirt, have a couple of beers, and watch television. Since he is *only* going to be with his wife, there is no need to put any extra zest into life.

Because of this mental attitude, careless couples settle into the senescence of marriage and begin the unfortunate process of marital disillusionment and "falling out of love." This mental attitude is responsible for many divorces as couples assume that once they marry, the task of living is resolved forever. In reality, marriage is an alive and dynamic relationship. The quality of the marital relationship is always in a state of flux, either improving or degenerating. It is unnecessary to ascribe a negative connotation to the concept "work." Our cultural bias dictating that work is arduous and therefore undesirable is, in many instances, unfounded. Many people find work to be rewarding, enriching, and enjoyable. The work of creating a successful marriage can be enjoyable. The happily married couple realizes that opportunity is hard to recognize if one is only looking for a lucky break.

Marriage is like the two oysters in a story by Kahlil Gibran. "Said one oyster to a neighboring oyster, 'I have a great pain within me. It is heavy and round and I am in distress.' And the other oyster replied with haughty complacence, 'Praise be to the heavens and to the sea, I am well and whole within and without.' At this moment, a crab was passing by and he said to the one who was well within and without, 'Yes, you are well and whole; but the pain that your neighbor bears is a pearl of exceeding beauty.' " It is the same with the marital relationship. Sticking to the task of marriage may sometimes be painful. Hopefully, the pain we experience will bring with it a pearl of exceeding beauty. This unwitting failure to look at marriage as a vocation is the primary problem facing modern couples.

Many couples use marriage as an excuse to stop working at a relationship. After marriage, many spouses cease trying to be loving and appealing to each other. After the first evening of a weekend workshop I conducted for engaged couples, I watched them drive away. Although some of the cars had bucket seats, the women sat close to their fiances. The next day, imagining their discomfort, I asked them how they were able to sit so close. The women explained, "We just sit between the two seats." It's difficult to imagine married couples going through this discomfort in order to sit next to each other. In fact, one generally assumes a couple is married if they are not sitting close. After about twenty years of marriage, we will find Tom and Peggy driving down the highway with Peggy huddled in her corner of the car. Because of her "arthritis," her coat will be wrapped around her shoulders and she will comment, "My, Tom, how far apart we've grown in these twenty years of marriage." In typical male fashion, Tom will comment, "Well, I haven't moved." However, couples have an alternate choice. They can be like Carol and Bill. A friend of Carol and Bill's sixteen year old daughter noticed they sat close to each other in the car and asked the daughter, "What's wrong with your parents?" This very alert young lady replied, "Well, you know, they're going together!" Married couples often forget that they are, indeed, still going together.

I once sat with a man on a plane who made several loving references to his wife. Because of the bad weather, he was concerned that he had asked her to meet him at the airport. As we walked down the ramp, he looked for his wife asking, "Where is my sweetheart?" Suddenly he saw her, turned to me saying, "There's my sweetheart, it's been nice talking to you." They rushed to embrace each other. This couple, in their early sixties, were not embarrassed to let the world know they were in love.

On the other hand, it is necessary to place mature married love into its proper perspective. Couples sometimes panic when they notice their relationship losing some of the qualities of romantic love. It is important for couples to distinguish between romantic and mature married love. They must realize that love is not instinctual. We become loving people by experiencing love. Couples begin their marriage with a love feeling. However, they arrive at mature married love as a result of solving the task of marriage. We continually try to explain love. However, we find that it is much like electricity—we really do not know what it is, but we know how it works. Rudolf Dreikurs explains, "We do know love. Every generation has had its poets and singers to praise it, its cynics and misanthropes to attack it, and its psychologists and philosophers to explain it. No one denies that love is, we argue only about what love is."[1] The resolution of this task is an important theme of this book.

Romantic love is a feeling that bells are ringing and that a roaring fire is burning inside of the lover. A young engaged man once asked me if I thought he was really in love. He explained, "It must be love! Whenever I see her, my heart pounds like a trip hammer. What could it be but love?" I suggested it could be love; however, it was also likely he was having a mild heart attack. As George Bernard Shaw explains, "People in love are under the influence of the most violent, most insane, most elusive, and most transient of passions and they are required to swear that they will remain in that excited, abnormal, exhausting condition until death do them part." Couples are unfair to themselves if they continue to want to have their hearts stormed by love. Dreikurs explains:

> Romantic love is a concept hard to give up. . . . We long wistfully to have our souls assaulted and conquered by some mysterious force against which we are powerless. And we are as loath to relinquish this concept as we were to give up the myths of our childhood. For many of us, the criterion of true love is that it be spiced with a dash of unhappiness, there should be just the right amount of heartache, sleeplessness, and inability to concentrate on one's work. Add to this just a grain of jealousy (more would spoil the brew) and one has the secret formula for romantic love.[2]

---

[1] Rudolf Dreikurs, *The Challenge of Marriage*, (New York: Duell, Sloan, and Pearce, 1946), p. 13.

[2] Ibid. p. 13.

Although romantic love is sometimes spoken of in a derisive manner, it must be recalled that it is a stage in the dynamic love relationship. A study by Graham B. Spanier[3] is one of the many which suggest that romanticism is not harmful to marriage relationships in particular or the family system in general. Difficulty is experienced when individuals do not separate the romantic from the realistic as necessary in real life marriage relationships.

Most people could not long survive in the excited and exhausted condition which emanates from romantic love. The temperature of love must simmer down so it can be lived with in both summer and winter. For instance, in the Orient, there is a different approach to married life which has been described in this manner: For the Oriental, marriage is like putting a kettle of cold water on a hot stove; for the American, too often, it is like putting a kettle of hot water on a cold stove. This points out the risk that rather than to substitute romantic love with the more comfortable state of mature married love, couples may settle into the senescence of marriage. Couples need to remember the importance of working at developing their love. Bernard Steinzor[4] explains, "Love does not spring willy-nilly from good intentions alone as Minerva sprang from the head of Zeus, but human love in all its forms requires painstaking cultivation, concentration, and the pursuit of knowledge—of the self and the other."

For the married couple, love is like a rose garden. The potential for beauty exists when the bushes are planted. However, if one intends to garner bouquets of beautiful flowers, the garden must be tenderly and lovingly cared for. Left to take care of itself, the potential beauty will never be

[3]Graham B. Spanier, "Romanticism and Marital Adjustment," *Journal of Marriage and the Family,* Vol. 34, No. 3, (August, 1972), pp. 481-487.

[4]Bernard Steinzor, *When Parents Divorce: A New Approach To New Relationships,* (New York: Pantheon Books, 1969), p. 237.

realized. It is the same with marital love. If it receives tender loving care, the couple will be able to enjoy the comfort and nurturance emanating from a loving marriage. Although many have written about the meaning and potential of marital love, the author especially appreciates the comments of Joseph and Lois Bird.[5] They explain that love becomes a foretaste of God's love and a binding union is fostered and created. The love has the potential for ecstasy as the couple comes to the realization of what it means to be totally known and possessed. They cite several descriptions of love contained in Scripture: Love was to be the new law, the law of Christ. (Galatians 6:2) In a truly Christian marriage, a man and a woman abandon their own individual lives and give themselves completely to one another, as Christ does to his Church, and together form one unit, living one new life. They are not only two in one flesh, but they are two in one life. The eminent psychiatrist, Harry Stack Sullivan, believed that, "When the satisfaction or the security of another person becomes as significant to one as is one's own satisfaction or security, then the state of love exists." This may be a variation of Paul's comments to the Corinthians:

> Love is patient; love is kind. Love is not jealous, it does not put on airs, it is not snobbish. Love is never rude, it is not self-seeking, it is not prone to anger; neither does it brood over injuries. Love does not rejoice in what is wrong, but rejoices with the truth. There is no limit to love's forbearance, to its trust, its hope, its power to endure.   (1 Corinthians 13:4)

Dietrich Von Hildebrand[6] explains, "In giving, we receive and in self-donation, our real self is given to us. The words of

---

[5]Joseph and Lois Bird, *The Freedom of Sexual Love,* (Garden City, New York: Doubleday and Company, Inc., 1967).

[6]Dietrich Von Hildebrand, "Marriage Is A Way Of Perfection," *Marriage In The Light of Vatican II,* (James T. McHugh, Ed. Washington, D.C.: Family Life Bureau, United States Catholic Conference, 1968), p. 131.

our Lord that 'he who loses his life will gain it' certainly refer to our ultimate surrender to Christ, but they apply analogously to all natural categories of love, especially to marital love." Also, in view of what will be discussed in later chapters, Hildebrand discusses the necessity. of concern for and love of oneself. He writes:

> The gift of self in marital love must be clearly distinguished from any depersonalizing absorption of the individual person by a collective. Just as the Christian's total gift of self to God is opposed to the depersonalizing ideal of dissolution of the individual's personal existence in a nirvana or in a pantheistic divinity, so, too, the gift of self in marital love is opposed to any absorption of the individual person whereby he would become only a means for, or part of, a collective.[7]

Rather than to discuss the concept of love *in toto,* it has only been intended to emphasize the dynamic nature of marital love and the necessity of looking at marriage as a task to be resolved, realizing that married love is the fruit of resolving the task of marriage.

Perhaps the concept of marriage as a task is best exemplified by a couple I met several years ago. At the conclusion of a weekend renewal, Karl thanked me for being with them. He went on to say that he and Claudia had been married for fifty years. He believed theirs was a fruitful and rewarding marriage. However, he explained they conceived of marriage as such a serious vocation that they found it necessary every year or two to set aside an evening or a weekend for a marriage retreat or renewal. He said that if they had not done this, he feared they would have fallen into some ruts and traps. Their marriage represented a powerful witness to the value of recognizing marriage as a vocation and the importance of working at developing married love. Married love is

---

[7]*Ibid.,* p. 131.

much like a diamond. A diamond is nothing but a glob of carbon—a glob of carbon that sticks to its job becomes a diamond. Marriage is the same. We must stick to the job of being married in order to realize that jewel of satisfaction that comes from true and married love.

CHAPTER 2

Marital Moments

In order to place into perspective the concepts of romantic and marital love, the senescence of marriage, and the value of viewing marriage as a task, it is necessary to be aware of the various moments in marriage. Aaron Rutledge explains that couples "expect marriage to be a combination of a religious conversion experience, a successful psychoanalysis, and a vacation in a tropical paradise."[1] In reality, no human experience can measure up to the expectations couples often establish for marriage. As a result of the unrealistic expectations, spouses frequently set themselves up for disenchantment.

William Lederer and Don Jackson suggest that our expectations of marriage are similar to those of the couple who prepared for a vacation in Florida. They packed clothes and equipment appropriate to the Florida climate. However, enroute to Florida, the plane was hijacked and they ended up in the Swiss Alps. Bikinis and golf clubs are out of place in the Swiss Alps. However, once one acclimates himself by getting winter clothing and ski equipment, the Swiss Alps are not such a bad place. It is the same with marriage—if we have a reasonable perspective of the moments in marriage, we re-

---

[1]Aaron L. Rutledge, *Pre-marital Counseling,* (Cambridge, Massachusetts: Schenkman Publishing Company, Inc., 1966), p. 5.

duce the possibility of disillusionment and the probability of being shattered by disenchantment.

Our marital life is occupied with three primary moments which, in my terminology, are the nitty-gritty or zilchy[2] moments, pizza and beer or recuperative moments, and ecstatic moments. In the following pages, I hope to demonstrate the dynamic inter-relationship of these moments. A pivotal thesis is that the ability to enjoy the recuperative and the ecstatic moments depends upon the ability to find meaning in the nitty-gritty moments.

Nitty-Gritty Moments

The nitty-gritty moments are filled with the kinds of things that need to be done to keep life together. Perhaps picking up the house, going off to work, changing diapers, shopping, and all the other "nutsy-boltsy" activities are not all that exciting. However, they are an essential part of a total life. Unfortunately, our society has developed an antagonistic attitude toward these activities. There is a strong suggestion that these everyday, have-to, coercive moments chain spouses to an unrewarding and unfulfilled existence. If one develops a broader view of daily activities, it may be realized that fulfillment consists not only of one type or set of experiences. Instead, fulfillment comes from living a multi-dimensional life which allows for variety and enrichment. On the other hand, fulfillment also requires the doing of "zilchy" activities. In fact, if we did not feel that it was "in" to look upon these activities as an insult to our individual integrity,

---

[2]The zilchy moments are those during which one does the necessary, routine activities of life that are not necessarily pleasant, but are necessary if life is to be held together. These are the frustrating or boring moments during which time we must have faith that "a better day is ahead."

we may find some inherent enjoyment in the doing of these projects. It is just possible that these activities could be enjoyed if approached in a positive manner. Even if it is difficult to find inherent pleasure in the accomplishment of these individual tasks, it is necessary to realize that they are what tie life together. In this way, one can see that if one is going to feel totally fulfilled, the accomplishment of "zilchy" tasks is a part of the fulfillment.

When the newly married couple experiences the initial pangs of disillusionment, they usually believe it necessary to do something more exotic with their lives. First, they may buy a boat and motor, water skis, and other paraphernalia for summer recreation. They get through the summer and the husband survives the fall by watching football on television. However, by early December they again sense a vague feeling of dissatisfaction. They slide through the winter with their "his and hers" snowmobiles. However, come March, they again feel vaguely uncomfortable and dissatisfied. Perhaps, then, they decide that a trip to a tropical paradise will solve their problems. They return and soon tire of showing their slides and the old feeling of dissatisfaction returns. The new furniture, the red carpeting for the bedroom, etc., doesn't solve their sense of disenchantment.

Rather than continue looking for answers outside themselves and believing that the answer lies in the world of erotica, couples must realize they are not being cheated if nitty-gritty activities occupy a greater share of their life. Perhaps the experience of marriage is much like that of Sir Alexander Fleming who discovered penicillin while working in a dusty old laboratory. A mold spore, blown in through a window, landed on a culture plate he was about to examine. Some years later, he was touring an up-to-date research lab, a gleaming air-conditioned, dust-free, super-sterile setting. "What a pity you did not have a place like this to work in," his guide said. "What you could have discovered in such surroundings!" "Not penicillin," Fleming observed dryly. Perhaps significant discoveries about marriage can be made in everyday "dusty" surroundings.

Pizza and Beer Moments

The second level of moments in marriage has to do with the recuperative moments in which we again do everyday kinds of things that seem to put zest into our system. These moments provide us with the encouragement to continue. They recharge us for the next day's or next week's work. The pizza and beer activities are perhaps the very simple experiences such as enjoying a sunset, a sunrise, a cloudy day, a rainy day, an evening of listening to music, etc. These are essentially the admission-free activities that revolve around sitting together, relaxing, and perhaps only enjoying a pizza and beer rather than a gourmet meal complete with soft lights and violins. During these refreshing moments, couples have an opportunity to realize that much happiness is lost because it does not cost anything.

Unfortunately, we live in a materialistic culture in which it is pumped into us that we, "need to take a sun break," "must get away from it all," or "you only go around once in this life, so you've got to grab all the gusto you can get." The underlying notion is that we cannot really find happiness in the nitty-gritty or recuperative moments we share together. One gets the idea that happiness is having what you want rather than wanting what you have. It seems that happiness must be bought and that it is something one can seek and not something within our immediate grasp. For instance, for her husband's birthday, one wife gift-wrapped boxes from each of the stores where they had charge accounts, and in each she put this message: "A gift has not been bought for you nor has it been charged to your account at this store." He said it was one of the best birthdays he ever had. It is necessary for the modern couple to confront this paganistic and hedonistic philosophy. Couples must resist the subliminal influence of a commercialized society.

It is frequently helpful for couples to examine some of the most treasured moments they have shared together or some of the most treasured moments from their own childhood. Spouses often discover that the most cherished moments were the very simple experiences they shared together such as a fall walk in the woods over crisp leaves, a bike ride, or an evening of cards with friends. They also find these simple experiences cost very little money.

Exotic Moments

It seems that many couples take one "exotic" vacation after the other or go from one "fabulous" restaurant to another. As we listen to their stories, we may become jealous. This envious feeling persists until it is realized that they represent the vacuous man described by Rollo May in his book, *Love and Will*. It suddenly dawns upon us that these people are not enjoying themselves. An in-depth conversation with them reveals they do not enjoy the nitty-gritty or the recuperative moments. If the exotic moments are to be memorable, a couple must develop the ability to enjoy the nutsy-boltsy and recuperative moments. If one has developed this ability, there is then the commensurate ability to enjoy the exotic moments which may occur once a year, once in five years, or once in a life-time. This may be the wonderful and problem-free vacation with or without the children, the beautiful reunion with one's family, or the trip to a tropical paradise. Of course, it must be recognized that people disagree as to what they consider to be exotic. Many parents explain that seeing their newborn child is an exotic moment. Others say the pizza and beer moments are exotic. Others find ecstasy in watching an opera and others find buying a new car to be a once in a life-time experience. People are free to describe for themselves what they consider to be zilchy, recuperative, and exotic.

Many couples have explained that it is difficult to create much erotica in marriage. This was discovered by one couple who celebrated their tenth anniversary by preparing a steak dinner by candlelight on their backporch. The porch shades were drawn, the charcoal glowed, the candles flickered, soft romantic music filtered through the air, and a bottle of champagne was being chilled in the scrub bucket. They danced together and were just sitting down to eat their steaks when the neighbor boy raced down the alley on his mufflerless motor cycle. They recovered from that shock when their seven year old son pulled up a chair beside them deciding he could not sleep and that it was much more fun to talk with Mom and Dad. It is moments like these that sometimes cause couples to believe that children are committed to breaking up marriages.

Perhaps the moments of marriage are best described in the following poem:

HAPPINESS

Happiness is the greatest paradox
in nature.
It can grow in any soil,
live under any conditions.
It defies environment.
It comes from within;
It is
the revelation of the depth
of the inner life as light
and heat proclaim the sun
from which they radiate.

Happiness consists not of
having but of being, not of
possessing but enjoying.
A martyr at the stake may have
happiness that a king on his
throne might envy.
Man is the creator of his
own happiness.
It is the aroma of a life lived
in harmony with high ideals.

For what a man *has* he may be
dependent on others;
what he *is*
rests with him alone.

Happiness is the soul's joy
in possession of the
intangible.
It is the warm glow of a heart
at peace with itself.

William George Jordan

Proclaiming A Positive Attitude

Another cultural bias complicating marriage is the popular game of putting down marriage. It is unpopular to talk about marriage in a positive and optimistic sense. It is more "in" to quip that "marriage is love, love is blind; therefore, marriage is an institution for the blind." It is also popular to say that, "all men are born free, but some get married." Apparently Socrates has said, "Whether you marry or not, you will live to regret it." This subtle pressure to speak negatively about marriage influences the attitude of young and old.

The portrayal of a positive attitude is especially difficult for the man who is about to be married. He is expected to act as though he is the victim and the prize that was captured. It is supposed that he has given up all his freedom and all of his friends and that he is entering into a ball and chain relationship. Marriage is described as the only institution in which the hunted pays for the license. One couple, after announcing their engagement, received a sympathy card.

The predicament of the prospective bride is almost as difficult. She is to be optimistic and is not permitted to harbor any doubts. She is congratulated when she announces the engagement whereas condolences are offered to the young man. However, it may be as difficult to be totally optimistic as it is to be negative. It is frightening to the prospective bride to find that all her concerns about marriage are brushed aside with the statement, "Oh, you have just the premarital jitters. You'll get over it." However, another phenomenon being noted in the age of liberation, is that the negative attitude is affecting women. They are coming to the point of treating prospective brides in a manner similar to that in which prospective grooms are treated.

It is necessary for those who work with the engaged to reassess the paganistic practice of bachelor parties. We do live in a transient and mobile age and old friends use opportunities such as weddings to renew the viability of their relationship. It is not objectionable for friends to use the auspicious occasion of a marriage to get together. On the other hand, the bachelor party serves as one of the rites of passage which, in their legitimate form, are unfortunately absent from our "waspish" (White, Anglo-Saxon, Protestant) society. This can be a passage away from old parental, family, and friendship ties to a new life and new relationships.

However, the mental attitude which suggests that the husband-to-be is giving up all of his freedom and needs his one last fling is objectionable. Perhaps a bachelor party is no more appropriate for the couple who are entering marriage than it would be for the person who is preparing for ordination to the ministry or for the person preparing to profess vows for the religious life. Usually people who are going to be ordained or who are going to profess vows go on a retreat prior to this important occasion. Perhaps the engaged should be encouraged to make a retreat rather than to have bachelor parties and bridal showers.

I was once in the barber shop when a young man announced he was going to be married that evening. The men in the shop responded in a conditioned way. They went into their usual refrain offering condolences. To this, the young man said, "That now makes the six hundredth person who has told me I am a sucker and a fool for getting married." The "old married men" enumerated their complaints about marriage and reminisced about what they would do if only they were twenty years younger. No one gave the groom an opportunity to protest and to say, "Hey, I happen to love this girl I'm going to marry and I'm looking forward to it."

After some while, I intervened in the conversation asking the married men if they were really all that unhappy. When they found they had permission to talk positively about marriage, they were able to identify what they liked about marriage and why they would not trade this vocation for any other walk of life. The prospective groom gave a sigh of relief and explained, "It's sure good to realize that some people like marriage."

If couples are to proclaim a positive witness for the sacrament and covenant of marriage, it is necessary to promulgate a positive attitude.

BIBLIOGRAPHY

Dreikurs, Rudolf. *The Challenge Of Marriage*. New York: Duell, Sloan, and Pearce, 1946.

> Dr. Dreikurs deals with the psychological and social factors which are responsible for our present day confusion in the problems of sex, love, and marriage.

Lederer, William J., and Jackson, Don D. *The Mirages of Marriage*. New York: W. W. Norton & Co., Inc., 1968.

> A profoundly helpful, incisive analysis of marriage in America. The authors present a systems concept. They deal with the marital relationship as it is.

Lee, Robert, and Casebier, Marjorie. *The Spouse Gap*. Nashville and New York: Abingdon Press, 1971.

> Many of us assume that if a marriage works for fifteen or twenty years that it is a lead pipe cinch. This just isn't true. Middlescence is a crisis period when couples may face some of their toughest battles: worry over kids and how to support them, aging parents who may need help, and the psychological and physiological problems which can crop up in the middle years. On top of all this, the marriage relationship itself may be showing signs of neglect. Just when couples need each other most, they find they're facing a spouse gap.

McHugh, James T., ed. *Marriage In The Light Of Vatican II*. Washington D.C.: Family Life Bureau, United States Catholic Conference, 1968.

> This is a commentary on the documents from Vatican II pertaining to the theology of marriage.

O'Neill, Nena, and O'Neill, George. *Open Marriage, A New Life Style For Couples*. New York: Evans Company, Inc., 1972.

Open Marriage is advertised as a book which describes a new life for couples.

Vollebregt, G. N. *The Bible On Marriage.* De Pere, Wisconsin: St. Norbert Abbey Press, 1965.

A short survey of the biblical data about the relationship of man and wife. An opinion of God's vision of marriage.

Section II

DISCOVERING THE SELF

CHAPTER 3

The Sensitive Self

The tendency of many who experience difficulty in married life is to look outside themselves for an explanation of the pain that is experienced. Generally, we want to blame our spouse, his parents, or his friends. It is seldom that spouses look within themselves for an explanation of the tension and difficulties that are experienced in marriage. Marriage requires the maturity exemplified in:

THE MAN IN THE GLASS

When you get what you want in your struggle for self
And the world makes you king for a day,
Just go to a mirror and look at yourself,
And see what that man has to say.

For it isn't your father or mother or wife
Whose judgment upon you must pass;
The fellow whose verdict counts most in your life
Is the one staring back from the glass.

You may be like Jack Horner and chisel a plum
And think you're a wonderful guy,
But the man in the glass says you're only a bum
If you can't look him straight in the eye.

He's the fellow to please, never mind all the rest,
For he's with you clear up to the end.
And you've passed your most dangerous, difficult test
If the man in the glass is your friend.

You may fool the whole world down the pathway of years
And get pats on the back as you pass,
But your final reward will be heartaches and tears
If you've cheated the man in the glass.

(Author unknown)

Our quest for happiness in marriage is aided if we look within ourselves and find that we like what we see. Acceptance of self precedes acceptance of spouse. Several studies suggest that people with low self-concepts also manifest low acceptance of others as well. Acceptance of self is expressed in Frederick Perls' comment that, "The crazy person says, 'I am Abraham Lincoln,' and the neurotic says, 'I wish I were Abraham Lincoln,' and the healthy person says, 'I am I and you are you.' "[1] Martin Buber expresses the same thought when he states, "If I am I because you are you and you are you because I am I; then I am not I and you are not you. But, if I am I because I am I and you are you because you are you; then we are people and we can talk."[2] Perls and Buber help us to see the meaning of the comment that mental health is the ability to do the best with what one has and to enjoy doing it. It is easier to express love and to be a loving person if one feels lovable. In this chapter, I will examine the concept of self-acceptance, explore some of the life experiences that make it difficult for us to be totally comfortable

[1] Frederick Perls, *Gestalt Therapy Verbatim*, (Lafayette, California: Real People Press, 1969), p. 40.

[2] Author not certain of exact quote and unable to find source.

with ourselves, and discuss the sensitive spots caused by these life experiences. In the next chapter, I will discuss the effect these sensitivities have upon the marriage relationship. In future chapters, I will examine the phenomenon of marital interaction, exploring the way in which we seek to change each other in marriage.

Spouses should seek to become acquainted with the most important person in their lives; that is, each spouse should become acquainted with himself. Sometimes we are like the character in the Pogo comic strip who commented, "I have seen the enemy and it is me." We go about our adult life with excess baggage. This baggage consists of past experiences which we have repressed and forgotten about. However, the baggage continues to weigh us down. It affects how we think about ourselves and the way in which we react to our spouse. Various traumatic life experiences are indelibly imprinted upon our psyche. Rather than seek to understand the impact these painful experiences have upon our present-day life, many of us brush them aside as archeological artifacts. George Santayana stated, "Those who do not know the past are doomed to relive it." It is important that we take the packs off our back, empty them out in front of us, and examine the baggage. If we examine the content of these past experiences, we may find they are, indeed, from the past, that times have changed, and that it is unnecessary to continue harboring the fears experienced when we were a relatively defenseless five or fifteen year old. If we examine the contents of these "garbage packs," we may be able to gain a new confidence in ourselves.

The thousands of couples I have seen in marital therapy and weekend seminars have demonstrated to me that many disagreements in marriage have little or nothing to do with present reality. A couple may disagree about finances, visits with in-laws, etc. After a moment of discussion, the initial

focus of the disagreement is lost and the couple find themselves enmeshed in a frustrating system of interaction in
which they cannot specifically identify the central issues
involved in their dispute. This frustrating situation is explained by the realization that we enter adult life after
experiencing various developmental traumas. Growth is not
an easy or nontraumatic experience. Various pains are in-
flicted upon us. We enter our adult life with various sensitive
spots and scars. Psychological and physical bruises are similar.
At one time or another, all of us have been physically
bruised. We soon forget the pain. However, if sometime later
someone accidentally bumps the bruised area, the pain may
be greater than that initially experienced. The person who
bumped us is dismayed that his unintentional nudge should
cause such pain. In order to place the present into perspective, we need to recall the initial bruise.

Our emotional sensitivities develop in much the same way
as our physical sensitivities. That is, we may have been
emotionally injured some years earlier. We feel no additional
pain until somebody nudges us in this sensitive spot. At this
point, we react strongly. The person who nudged our emotions is dismayed and unable to understand our reaction.
Again, unless we are able to place the past into perspective
and understand why this is a sensitive issue for us, we blame
the present reality rather than understand that our super-
reaction results from previously experienced trauma.

This gives us an idea of the way marital conflicts develop.
Couples become involved in a system in which they are
"kicking" each other in their emotionally sensitive spots.
Some of the developmental experiences have been good and
rewarding and have left us with psychological reservoirs of
strength. As Saul Bellow says in *Mr. Sammler's Planet,*
"Everyone needs memories; it keeps the wolf of insignifi-
cance from the door." On the other hand, the mind is like a

sponge. Some people wish they could squeeze theirs out once in a while to get rid of the stuff they don't need. Some of our developmental experiences have been good and rewarding; others have been damaging. We realize that our lives are shaped by those who love us as well as those who refuse to love us. These damaging or negative experiences leave us with sensitive and vulnerable spots.

The phenomenon of sensitizing is exemplified by the husband who is greeted by his wife when he returns from school. She asks, "How did school go today, Bob?" He replies, "Get off my back about school! Quit bugging me! It went the way it usually goes! Now leave me alone!" Obviously Bob overreacted. In reality, he did not hear his wife ask him about his day in school. When she asked him about school, he heard the voice of his parents from the past whom he could never please. If he came home with four A's and a B, they nagged him for neglecting the subject in which he got the B. His wife's question about school struck his sensitivities about the pressure placed on him by his parents.

We enter into adult life with super-sensitive radar screens. At one time, one of the United States Air Force radar stations called an alert because the crew noticed a flight of enemy Migs entering into U. S. territory. A squadron of U. S. fighter planes went into the air only to take on a flock of birds. The radar system had been too sensitive and misidentified a flock of birds for a flight of enemy Migs. It is the same with the super-sensitive radar systems all of us have developed. We identify an insignificant, or perhaps even pleasant event, as being something significant or traumatic. This human propensity reminds one of Sir William Osler's pithy observation that, "Twenty years of making the same mistake does not constitute experience." This is very similar to Henri Bergson's comment that, "The tools of the mind become burdens when the environment which made them necessary no longer exists." However, if we become aware of our sensitivities, we can build in a correction for our personal radar systems.

During the course of a marriage renewal weekend, I jokingly commented that there was no need for a husband to argue with his wife as it was his word against thousands of hers. During the break, a very angry lady approached me. She explained that I was nothing but a male chauvinist who was putting down women. She talked at me for a few moments and left the session in tears. Since I do not believe that I am a male chauvinist, I thought she over-reacted. Apparently my remark struck a sensitive spot within her. Her radar system misidentified my comment and she became needlessly upset.

We spend our developmental life learning a particular language of behavior. We learn ways in which to defend ourselves, to express ourselves, and ways in which to repress our emotions. Essentially, we learn a life style. In many instances, a life style evolves which contributes to our happiness. However, in some instances, we learn a life style which contributes to our unhappiness. The sensitive spots that we have discussed become a part of our language and life style. We may go for months or years without being hit in any of these sensitive spots—we react with pain and anguish. At this time, we retreat to an old language or behavior style not realizing that language or behavior style is no longer necessary.

I developed the notion of a language some years ago while talking with a couple who, as adults, moved to the United States from Germany. They had lived in the United States for some years and spoke English fluently. During one of the interviews, the husband became angry with his wife and began speaking in German. When he finished speaking, I asked him to translate what he had said. He wondered why I had not understood him. I explained he had drifted off into German. He was amazed, did not realize that he had reverted to his native tongue, and then proceeded to translate what he had said. This reminded me of the many immigrants to the United States who spoke fluent English until they hit their thumb with a hammer. At that point of crisis, they drifted off into their native tongue and "called for God's assistance."

It is the same with our life style (language of behavior). We may adopt a new language and a new behavior for adult life, but at a time of crisis, we may revert to the language of an earlier age. The marital relationship presents us with many crises. It is essential for couples to understand the way in which they present crises for each other, causing each other to revert to an earlier language.

These sensitivities affect marital conflict in various ways. For instance, a woman may be so frightened of her husband's moods that she literally trembles at his slightest expression of anger. Because of her over-reaction, he doesn't know how to express his own feelings. Actually, the problem does not lie between them. Because of the many violent arguments his wife saw between her parents, she developed a super-sensitivity to any expression of anger. When her husband becomes angry, she reacts to it in the same way she reacted to her father's uncontrollable rages. It is essential for this woman to allow for a corrective factor in her radar system. Whenever she is faced with an expression of anger, she must remind herself that she has the tendency to over-react. She must them seek to judge the anger in terms of present reality rather than past memories.

In his book, *I'm O.K.; You're O.K.*, Thomas Harris[3] explains that the mind is like a computer bank. We have many computer tapes stored in our mind. When certain events occur, the tapes reel off and we recall some of the same feelings and emotions we experienced when the tapes were first registered and stored in the bank. Many of us have had

---

[3]Thomas Harris, *I'm O.K.; You're O.K.*, (New York and Evanston: Harper and Row, 1969).

then experiencing various emotions which we did not really understand. For instance, we may hear a song which elicits the experience of being exposed to a particular stimulus and certain emotions which are not explainable by what is going on in the present reality. If we jog our memory, we may find that we heard that song some years earlier. At the time of the original recording, various experiences and emotional reactions were associated with the song. When we hear the song years later, those same emotions are recalled.

The stimulus of a certain event causes the computer bank to begin whirring away until it comes to the tape that has recorded the emotional reactions to similar earlier experiences. For instance, earlier in my life I participated in sports. One of the associations was the distinctive disinfectant used in locker rooms. In my adult life, I find that whenever I smell that disinfectant, I get the same butterflies which I experienced prior to athletic events. Also, a couple of years ago, my wife and I decided to go on an economy kick. Part of this involved my riding a motorscooter to save on car expenses. This worked fine until I "wiped out" on the scooter. In the present reality, I find that when I see somebody riding on a motorscooter, I develop the same discomfort and sick feeling that I had for a couple days after my traumatic accident.

Various present day stimuli elicit certain emotional responses recorded at the time of an earlier reality. The responses may have been stored for several years. This phenomenon has significant implications for marital interaction. Each spouse serves as a stimulus to the other. We cause each other's computer bank to begin whirring. Various emotional reactions are elicited which may not be well understood by ourselves or by our spouse.

For instance, if a wife begins to cry, becomes angry, or becomes otherwise upset, the husband may sit back in amazement not knowing what he has done to cause an emotional reaction. In fact, she may not actually hear what her husband has said or is saying. The stimulus sets off her emotional reactions. She is easily confused as to what is present and past reality. We need to realize that our mind and the messages we receive become very garbled. It is necessary that we become aware of what kind of experiences and consequent emotions are stored in our computer bank.

When we begin to feel angry or uneasy or dissatisfied, it is time to look at ourselves. These are the times when we may begin to act in a reflex manner. We may be reacting in a way in which we were conditioned to react, failing to realize that it may no longer be necessary to react with fear, anger, or panic. Because of these reflex reactions and the difficulty many have sorting out the "garbage packs," they retain and operate upon the basis of irrational notions about themselves and others. Although no one can explain why people react differently to the same developmental experiences, an understanding of these experiences and their impact helps us understand why we are who we are. For instance, two brothers a year apart in age were reared by neglectful, alcoholic, abusive, and inconsistent parents. The one brother worked his way through high school and college, married, and created a beautiful marriage and family life. When people asked him how he turned out so well, he explained, "I experienced so much abuse while growing up that I decided my life would be different than that of my parents." On the other hand, his brother dropped out of high school, never held a job for long, and was in continual trouble. People asked him why he was not like his brother and he explained, "I'm only doing what I was taught to do."

In spite of Hitler, Freud, and the Jesuits' comment: "Give me your child until he is seven and then do with him what you want," we realize that we cannot predict with certainty how people will react to developmental experiences.

The chain reaction effect of the sensitization process is exemplifed by Peter and Jane. Jane came from a family in which her father was dominated by Jane's paternal grandmother. This domination upset the entire family and was most upsetting to Jane. On the other hand, her husband's father was dominated by his own mother. Peter thought this was emasculating. Peter and Jane made unconscious decisions. Jane decided that no man should be dominated by his mother. She was not going to have an interfering mother-in-law. On the other hand, Peter decided he was not going to be dominated by his wife as was his father. Peter and Jane entered marriage with these sensitivities. We need to recall, Jane unconsciously decided the mother-in-law had absolutely no place in the marriage of her adult son. Jane reacted vehemently to even the mother-in-law's most innocuous suggestion. She insisted that she and her husband have absolutely nothing to do with his parents. Although Peter did not want to be dominated by his mother, neither did he want to be dominated by his wife. He resented her vehement and authoritative stand. As much as the mother-in-law's involvement struck at Jane's sensitivities, her authoritarian stand hurt Peter. It was not until the couple placed past and present reality into perspective that they were able to deal effectively with each other. In a sense, the worst boss anyone can have is a bad habit. In many respects, these reflex reactions are bad habits caused by fears which are no longer necessary.

I do not believe we can erase from our mind the impact of these previous experiences. The sensitivities we have developed may remain as sensitive issues. On the other hand, we can learn to identify them as sensitive issues, realize that we have the propensity to over-react, and then seek to control our reaction when we are faced with these sensitive experiences. We will only be frustrated if we expect that the impact of these experiences will totally disappear. Instead, we should develop the ability to recognize our sensitive spots. This enables us to control our reactions before they mushroom and avalanche completely out of control. The development of this type of insight is not easy. However, to be just and loving, spouses must concentrate on the problems of life with another. We must seek to gain knowledge of ourselves as well as of the person we love and cherish. In the words of the poet Pasternak, "To live life to the end is not a childish task." I do not suggest that we crucify ourselves between the two thieves of regret for yesterday and fear of tomorrow. I ask only that we understand yesterday so it is not repeated tomorrow.

In the next chapter I will build upon the sensitization concept introduced here. I will discuss various syndromes caused by particular developmental experiences. I will also discuss the effect these syndromes have upon marital interaction.

CHAPTER 4

Your Past Is Showing

The principle guideline involved in understanding super-sensitivities is to realize that whenever one's reaction is "too much," it is an indication that something from the past is being resurrected and that the couple is dealing with the impact of past rather than present reality.

We enter into marriage with a closet full of skeletons—upsetting past experiences. We then proceed to interact with each other in such a way that we rattle each other's closet and shake the skeletons about. I ask that we become aware of what causes our door to be rattled as well as the way in which we rattle the door of our spouse. This task reminds one of Carl Sandburg's comment, "Life is like an onion; you peel it off one layer at a time, and sometimes you weep."

It is helpful for couples to learn to distinguish between problems and conflicts. Problems are experienced by most couples and are on a conscious level. Many couples experience problems with in-laws, finances, child-rearing practices, etc. A problem is a phenomenon which a couple can face together. It is a problem *for* them and not *between* them. A conflict is an issue *between* a couple rather than *for* them. A conflict is generally on a pre-conscious or unconscious level. Conflicts are generally not understood until we come to grips with our own sensitivities and the way in which these are affected in marriage. When we have a super-reaction, we can generally be assured that we are involved in a conflict issue. Being *too* upset about something is a super-reaction. In other words, crying *too* much, being *too* angry, or *too* anxious are super-reactions. A super-reaction is an indication that a sensitivity has been struck. Another indication of a conflict is when the issue remains relatively unresolved. That is, when we continually hassle about one thing or the other and it appears impossible to reach an amicable solution. Another indication that we are involved in a conflict issue is when we bring all sorts of falderal into the conversation. If we bring up previously unresolved arguments, the weight of our spouse, the repair of the home, or other issues not related to the present problem, we have some indication we are involved in a conflict situation in which we are seeking to protect the very core of our life.

The only way in which a conflict issue can be resolved is by developing an understanding of the source of the conflict. That is, how did we become sensitive to one thing or the other and what would be an effective way in the present reality of dealing with traumatic past reality. For instance, if a couple continually argue about how much contact they should or should not have with in-laws and when this becomes a conflict between them rather than a problem for them, they will have to examine the meaning that parents and in-laws have in their psychic make-up. If finances become a conflict issue, it becomes necessary to understand the etiological phenomenon behind the conflict. Sometimes a wife's chronic complaint that there is not enough money may actually be a disguised expression for the hostility she feels toward her husband and an effort to emasculate him. A husband's hoarding of the family income may be an expression of his inability to share as well as an expression of his need to control and dominate.

Perhaps we can best continue to gain an understanding of the present day influence of past experiences by discussing various syndromes which are manifested by spouses in marriage. Because of these syndromes (sensitivities), couples become a source of pain to each other. They then continue to live a painful existence which would be unnecessary if the past were placed into perspective.

People Are No Darn Good

This misanthropic individual fears people and avoids intimate contact. If both husband and wife suffer from this particular syndrome, they may avoid intimacy and marriage may be neither painful or rewarding. On the other hand, if one spouse places a premium upon involvement with others, the couple begins to strike at each other's sensititivites. The fearful spouse feels the other spouse is unloving when he insists they get together with friends. In contrast, the spouse who places a premium upon involvement with others feels rejected and believes that the other spouse doesn't want to be out with him or her. In order to understand this individual, we must seek to comprehend the reasons the syndrome develops. The misanthrope resists contact with other people preferring a "quiet evening at home" to contact with other couples or friends. If the other spouse is a gregarious and outgoing individual, he may become upset that they never go out. Whereas, the spouse with this particular syndrome cannot understand why the other spouse would coerce or force him or her into doing something so painful. Rather than to simply be disgusted that the reluctant spouse doesn't understand that new lands cannot be discovered unless one has the courage to lose sight of the shore, the gregarious spouse must understand why the other wants to avoid people. We cannot understand another person unless we have walked in their shoes. Rather than to fight about this and make it a problem between them, it is better to understand why the one spouse wants to avoid people. The root of this syndrome often lies in the past and is based upon previously experienced trauma where people have proven to be hurtful rather than helpful. This is well exemplified in the ditty:

> When everyone cannot join in the laughter
> When something sacred is made to appear funny
> When some heart carries away an ache,
> It's a poor joke.
>
> (Author Unknown)

Most of us have been the victims of poor jokes. However, some people have been so victimized that they have decided to write off people.

I recall an attractive woman in her mid-thirties who conceived of herself as a horrible and ugly person. When she looked in the mirror, she did not see herself as an attractive woman. Instead, she saw the reflected image from some twenty years ago when she was struggling through high school as the victim of all the cruel jokes students thrust upon each other. She was teased because of the clothes she wore, the home in which she lived, the side of the tracks from which she came. The boys often grabbed her and locked her in her locker. She carried around this old baggage and had summarily decided to reject people. She did not realize that yesterday is not today.

Perhaps all of us can recall the student who was the scapegoat of the class. I recall the girl who was our scapegoat throughout elementary school. We nicknamed her trash-can. Whenever she walked by, we held our noses and exclaimed, "There goes trash-can." This was "funny" to everyone except the scapegoat.

A man I saw several years ago is indelibly imprinted upon my mind. He was strikingly handsome and in his mid-forties. However, he was a recluse. As a child, he had "elephant ears" and was the brunt of many jokes. His peers teased him exclaiming, "Hey, Tom, the ball is up on the roof. Why don't you fly up and get it?" His ears were not surgically corrected until he finished high school. In the present reality, whenever someone greeted him saying, "Good morning, Tom," he did not hear what was being said in the present reality. Instead, he heard voices from the past saying, "Hey, Tom, fly up and get our ball."

The impact of these developmental experiences dramatically struck me some years ago when I attended our ten year high school reunion. It was possible to identify the people who had been left on the fringe of things during their high school years and those for whom adolescence had been a particularly painful experience. They may have been the ones who, as adolescents, were particularly uncoordinated, had acute cases of acne, straight up and down figures, etc. Objectively, their physical appearance had changed significantly. However, it was evident that when they looked in the mirror before leaving for the reunion, they did not see themselves as they were in present reality. Instead, the image reflected was that of a person some ten years earlier who felt left out and insecure. They were desperately in need of a new mirror and a more accurate perception of themselves.

Since that initial reunion, I have talked with many people who explained that they never will or never would attend a high school reunion. They say the experience was or would be too painful and they did not want to relive that trauma. Avoidance of high school reunions and old friends may be advisable. On the other hand, I wonder if one might simply look at himself in a new way. In many instances, we are making judgments about ourselves that are based upon irrelevant data. The judgments are based upon experiences that occurred some ten, fifteen, twenty, or thirty years earlier in our life. We fail to take into account that we have new data upon which to judge ourselves. We may have changed physically, our personalities may have been modified, and our capabilities and capacities may have blossomed. However, we often fail to recognize this. Therefore, we continue to make judgments that are based upon teen-age experiences.

Narcissus

Narcissus believes that he is the center of the universe and all must revolve around him. This is the individual who, when he and his future wife announce their engagement to his mother, the mother looked at the girl and said, "Oh, dear, you are so very lucky! He is a most satisfactory son." At that point, the fiance looked at the mantle and noticed that the mother had a vigil light burning under the picture of her dearly beloved son. His mother's veneration of him suggests how he became narcissistic.

Narcissus cannot imagine that anyone would be displeased with him. He wants to be the center of attention. He is surprised whenever anyone disagrees with him. He expects to get his own way. He arrives an hour late for a meeting and is offended that the meeting started without him. As suggested above, Narcissus was brought up to believe that he was the most important person in the universe. He internalized this feeling and brought it into marriage. It is difficult to be married to Narcissus. It is not easy for him to share or to be understanding of others. It is difficult to live with someone who needs to have everything directed toward himself.

Guilty Milty (or Millie)

Guilty Milty was taught to believe that he could do nothing that was simply wrong or mischievous. Any offense was considered terrible and awful and one that would incur the eternal wrath of God. He was not only threatened with a spanking but with the eternal fires of damnation. Milty was reared in such a way that he continually wondered what he would do wrong. He is obsessed with his many faults and has little or no idea of his assets. As an adult, he is hampered by his guilt feelings. He fears most anything he does is wrong. He fears what he might do today and is paralyzed by guilt feelings from the past.

Guilty Milty needs to get the past out in front of him and examine the educative experiences that caused him to internalize this horrendous feeling of guilt. He needs to realize this is a different age and some of the educative experiences instilled in him by parents or religious educators were either erroneous or misdirected. He needs to come to grips with the impact of the New Testament which is based upon love and forgiveness rather than upon punishment. It is essential that he find some way in which the past can be placed into perspective so he does not continue to punish himself for past deeds, both real and imagined.

Don't Shove All That Religion Down My Throat

Somewhat at the opposite extreme of Milty and Millie is the individual who regurgitates most religion. He is reacting to a religion that was taught to him in a by-gone era. He forgets that the approaches utilized in conveying religious education have been modified. This is the individual who may be kicking over all traces of the past. He has little or no sympathy for the religious tradition which he has inherited. He typically throws the baby out with the bath. Rather than to place past religious experiences into a perspective consistent with present reality, he may reject the entire concept of religion. While discussing this syndrome during workshops, I have often asked whether or not the education to which many of us were subjected was all that harmful and if the damage was so irreversible. Several participants have had super-reactions to my comments. They have angrily exclaimed that the education was irrevocably damaging. Their over-reaction is evident. Apparently the religion, which had once played an important role in their life, was rammed down their throats. They are presently regurgitating it by their antagonistic and rejecting attitudes toward their heritage. I have often noticed that modern churches are being attacked by some who are still acting out the anger they have toward the religious education of an earlier age. Many, after achieving the demanded changes, still desert their church.

On the other hand, some have not kicked over some of the traces which need to be placed into perspective. I saw one woman in treatment who experienced a difficult childhood with her alcoholic father. Her teachers explained to her that she was very lucky that God loved her so much that he was giving her this cross to bear. In her adult life, she married, had a very fine husband, three lovely children, her life was going very nicely, and yet she was extremely anxious. As we explored her feelings, we realized that now that things were going well, she feared God no longer loved her.

Men (Or Women) Are No Good

Men and women frequently enter into marriage with underlying and unconscious feelings of hostility or fear toward people of the opposite sex. The explanation for the feelings of hostility is generally found when one begins to understand the quality of the relationship the person shared with his opposite-sexed parent. Again, this spouse may not realize the extent to which this language is imbedded within him until a crisis point is reached in the marriage. A wife may have been taught by her mother that men are terrible and awful creatures who do dastardly deeds to sweet young maidens. By and large, this thought remains unconscious until some behavior on the part of her husband activates her computer. At this point, she recalls voices from the past, misidentifies the present behavior of her husband, and reaffirms, within her unconscious mind, that men really are no good. In reality, his behavior may not justify affirmation of that old recording instilled in her by her mother. However, in a time of crisis, that recording is heard loud and clear. The husband may be very confused by his wife's strong reaction to his "minor transgression."

As a result of what was taught by his father or even the behavior he saw manifested by his mother, a husband may develop some of the same sensitivities toward women. That was true with Peter and Jane who were mentioned in the last chapter.

One young man tried desperately to find a girl of whom his mother approved. His mother rejected one girl after the other. A friend suggested he find a girl who was just like his mother. The friend thought the mother would approve of someone who was just like her. The young man saw his friend some months later and explained he had finally found a girl who was exactly like his mother. The friend was very congratulatory exclaiming, "I suppose now you will be getting married." The young man replied, "No, now my father does not approve of her."

Also, we tend to look to the same-sexed parent as a source of sexual identification. That is, we develop our idea of the role of masculinity and femininity from our father and mother.

Sex role identification is relatively uncomplicated if we have a positive relationship with the same-sexed parent and if we consciously want to be like him or her. Sexual identification becomes difficult if we reject the sex role model established by the same-sexed parent. If there is no desire to emulate the role which is presented, the young boy or girl is left adrift. Life is somewhat less complex if one knows what he wants to be and who he wants to be like. If one knows only what he does not want to be or what he does not want to be like, the development of a positive sense of sexual identity is complicated. It is like shopping for a wedding gift when one knows only what he does not want to buy. It is much easier if one knows what he's looking for. If we realize that we have a diffuse sense of sexual identity, it becomes necessary to review the quality of our relationship with the same-sexed parent. Realization that an identity model has been rejected helps us understand the diffuseness of our sexual identity. With this realization, we become able to look for positive models with whom we can identify and to develop a comfortable sexual identity.

Stay Away Closer

This aloof spouse has some of the same feelings as the one who has a diffuse sense of sexual identity or who has an unrecognized hostility toward the opposite sex. This is a frustrating syndrome. Yet, it is one of the more common phenomena noticed in modern marriage. The Stay Away Closer spouse desires a close relationship and yet fears intimacy. With this syndrome, we frequently find a history of aloof and distant relationships within the family of origin. It is also noticed that the parents may have reacted negatively to efforts on the part of the developing child to become intimate. As a result of repeated rejection or acts of indifference, the developing child begins to realize that it is safer to keep one's distance. This particular syndrome is described by Lee and Casebier.[1]

The syndrome is particularly frustrating as the spouse consciously feels that he or she wants to become intimate (not only in a sexual sense, but in the larger psychological and emotional sense); yet, there is usually some reason to

---

[1]Robert Lee and Marjorie Casebier, *The Spouse Gap*, (Nashville and New York: Abingdon Press, 1971).

justify backing away. Until the cause of the problem is understood, it becomes impossible for a couple to deal with the fact that they never seem to be tuned in on the same frequency.

A typical example of this phenomenon is Helen. During her fifteen years of marriage, Helen developed a phobic fear of pregnancy and a sense of disgust with intercourse. To understand her reactions, it was necessary to be aware of the reality of her past experiences. It was not enough to reassure her that there was little risk involved in pregnancy and that giving birth to new life was a beautiful experience. It was of little value to discuss the advantages of a meaningful sexual relationship. Any positive explanations were contradicted by the overwhelming impact of previous reality. The marital relationship between Helen's parents was horrendous. Her mother was treated as an object of primitive fecundity. The mother taught Helen that men were aggressive creatures who took unfair advantage of girls. The phrase, "What more can you expect of them?" was commonly heard. Her peers teased her about the large family from which she came asking how much fun her dad had in bed. As if these experiences were not enough, they were topped off by a horrible honeymoon experience which reaffirmed all that she had been taught to believe throughout the years. The accumulation of these experiences caused Helen to develop a fear of intimacy. Yet, she had the desire for closeness and intimacy that is shared by most humans. Her husband needed to understand that people who need love the most are the hardest to love. The person suffering from this syndrome is building walls and defenses so as not to be hurt. Unless the past is understood, it is quite unclear as to just what they fear. Also, the person is unaware of what he is missing as a result of his fears. This individual operates contrary to Robert Frost's advice: "Do not build a wall until you know what you are walling in and what you are walling out."

One of the common conflicts related to the Stay Away Closer syndrome is the conflict between independence and dependence which is shared by so many spouses. A conflict between dependence and independence causes a spouse to accuse people of not caring or of not getting close enough. However, when people become emotionally intimate, the wall builder finds something wrong with the closeness or accuses the other of only being interested in sex. As mentioned before, something always goes wrong and the need for intimacy is always frustrated.

It is necessary for spouses to examine their feelings about dependence and independence and the need for affection as compared with the need to remain aloof and distant. Spouses must gain some understanding of why they feel as they do about closeness or intimacy as compared with their feelings about distance and aloofness. The various popular philosophical revolutions as exemplified by the women's liberation movement, "do your thing," "each individual must decide for himself," etc., have caused many spouses to place a premium on independence rather than to come to grips with a concept of interdependence which allows for intimacy. Whereas engaged couples formerly commented that they were afraid of loneliness, many engaged couples now comment that their greatest sensitivity is people telling them what to do. Couples need to realize that being independent or dependent is not a challenge of consequence. The important challenge is to develop a sense of interdependence. In marriage, spouses cannot be islands unto themselves. In a sense, spouses need a declaration of interdependence. Marriage is a relationship in which the independence is equal, the dependence mutual, and the obligation reciprocal. It is a relationship in which it is all right to need each other. Indeed, a marriage may succeed or fail in direct relation to the extent to which the spouses need each other. The person laboring under the burden of the Stay Away Closer syndrome has failed to come to grips with the concept of interdependence. It would be nice if couples could follow the advice of Camus:

> Don't walk behind me, I may not lead,
> Don't walk in front, I may not follow,
> Walk beside me and be my friend.
> Do you agree?

In many marriages, both spouses suffer from the Stay Away Closer syndrome. In this relationship, it is as though there is a door on each side of the jamb. A short chain is attached between the doors. The chain allows one spouse to open the door in order to permit intimacy. The opening of that door automatically closes the door of the other spouse. After one spouse's door is closed for a while, he may decide to open his door. As he does that, the door of the other spouse is closed. It is as though there was a collusive agreement to prevent intimacy. They may each open the door but there is never enough room to permit intimacy. The frustration continues as each thinks he has opened himself up and that the other has closed the door.

Eggshell Syndrome

The Eggsheller fears upsetting the apple cart and causing problems. Life for him is similar to walking around on eggshells. He operates upon the premise of "peace at any price." He fears telling his spouse about any disagreement he may have with her. He internalizes all feelings of hostility explaining to himself, "It really doesn't matter." He is like Edith Bunker, the wife of Archie on the popular *All In The Family* television series. Whenever Archie asks Edith what she wants to do, her response is generally, "Whatever you would like, Archie." She expresses no opinions fearing she will upset someone. After several years, the Eggsheller is stoop-shouldered from bearing the responsibility for "world peace."

In seeking to understand this syndrome, we generally find the Eggsheller was reared in a family in which there was never a minor emergency. If the salt and pepper were not on the table, one or the other parent may have reacted as though the entire meal was burned. An improperly prepared meal could be cause for turning over the table. This syndrome develops as the person decides that he wants to avoid confrontation. He does everything possible to avoid causing trouble. He may hide and stay out of everyone's way.

Marriage to the Eggsheller is difficult as one never really knows the genuine feelings of the spouse. The Eggsheller tries desperately to please people. At some point, he must come to grips with the fact that he cannot be somebody else just for the sake of another person. He has a diffuse sense of his identity and tries on different identities as a person might try on different hats or suits in order to find out what is pleasing to other people.

The Hot Retort

At the opposite extreme of the Eggshell Syndrome is the Hot Retort. This person has decided he has taken enough blame. He develops a defensive attitude and shoots back from the hip. He seems unable to tolerate criticism and must always be right. It is difficult to live with this individual because he walks around as though he were encased in steel and as though there were little barbs jutting out from his armor. The Retorter frequently misinterprets innocent comments as criticisms. The Hot Retorter is the person to whom the other spouse always seems to be explaining himself and apologizing for this or that.

The Hot Retorter is comfortable in realizing that he is endowed with greater wisdom than anyone else. There is nothing he can be taught and nothing he can learn from anyone. He operates upon the premise that, "Even if I'm wrong, I'm right." This is the man who says to his wife, "If you agree with me, we are both right, if we disagree, *you* are wrong." This is the person who may have offended someone, begins to apologize, and within a couple of minutes is blaming the person to whom he is apologizing for causing him to do something offensive. The Hot Retorter concludes an apology by saying, "I wish you wouldn't do those things that make me so angry and cause me to act in a way in which I do not want to behave."

In seeking to understand the developmental history of the Retorter, we frequently find he has emulated a type of behavior presented to him by one or the other of his parents. An equally plausible explanation is that he may have been blamed for various and sundry things throughout the course of his childhood. Halfway through adolescence, he decides he has absorbed enough blame to last a lifetime. It seems he makes a decision that from that day forth he will accept no more blame. It is difficult to be married to someone encased in steel or someone who makes you feel as though you are always wrong.

I'll Do It Tomorrow

This is a very common syndrome. The "Tomorrower" is continually making lists. Men usually make their lists on Friday afternoon. The lists are neat and include all the husband is going to do during the weekend. Wives tend to make out their lists on Sunday evenings. There are all of the jobs that are going to be done during the week. The lists are neat, all inclusive, but somehow or other things never get done. The next week, the list is very neatly revised. Tomorrow never really seems to come.

In seeking to understand the "Tomorrower," we can generally look at his developmental years and find he could seldom do anything that gained his parent's approval. They believed that, "A job worth doing at all is a job worth doing well." Adolescents frequently decide, "O.K., I won't do it at all." This may be a reasonable solution for a fifteen year old who finds it is impossible to please his parents. However, the behavioral pattern is dysfunctional for the thirty-five year old.

It is interesting that many people reach their maximum level of inefficiency when they are visited by their parents. It is as though all the old recordings are being replayed. They seem to be hearing, "Can't you do anything right?" "You're just in the way! It's easier to do it myself!" The various recordings can go on *ad infinitum*. Frequently, children suffer the consequences of a self-fulfilling prophecy. In other words, if they are expected to fail or to fall short of expectations, they will fail and fall short of expectations. When they are visited by their parents, they seem to fall back into this old trap.

After hearing me explain this phenomenon, one forty-year-old man explained that he could now understand why he always seemed to mess things up whenever he tried, as an adult, to help his father with anything. He was an accomplished handyman who remodeled his recreation room and kept things in good repair. However, whenever he tried to help his father, something or other would go wrong. For instance, the forty-year-old son was helping his father paint the black trim of the father's newly stuccoed home. Somehow or other, he managed to spill a full can of paint down the side of the stucco. He went on to give several examples of something going wrong when, even as an adult, he sought to help his father.

The "Tomorrower" frequently operates under the assumption that, "If I really set my mind to it, I can do it." "It" may be vocational training, finishing the last year of college, a graduate degree, a different job, a job promotion, a household task, etc. Underneath the facade of confidence, he has an overwhelming fear that he cannot do as he claims. The protest of competence grants him a sense of integrity and the rationalization that permits him the opportunity to not come to grips with himself. If he really sat down to start or complete the task, he would have to face up to the reality of his competence, i.e., he may or may not be able to do the job. His statement, "If I really set my mind to it, I can do it," easily becomes a cop-out for never having to come to grips with what he cannot do.

It must also be remembered that the "Tomorrower" can be afflicted with a massive dose of "Not OK-ness" which causes him to follow a life script in which he must reinforce the Not OK life position. The failure to get things done unconsciously reinforces the Not OK-ness, but consciously provides him with the rationalization necessary to maintain the needed degree of integrity. He is following the deeply ingrained prophecy that he cannot do anything right.

The Eternal Pessimist

The Eternal Pessimist lives by "Murphy's Law" which states: "What can go wrong will go wrong." Each time he drops his toast, it lands butter side down. The Eternal Pessimist is like an accident waiting to happen. He has a sour outlook on life. He questions his worth and value. He always wonders when the roof is going to fall in. He explains, "When my ship comes in, there will probably be a dock strike." The Pessimist believes disaster is just around the corner. He knows that if he just waits long enough, something is certain to go wrong. Whereas the optimist gets up with the sun and says,

"Good morning, Lord!", a pessimist gets up and says, "Good Lord, morning!"

The Pessimist seems unable to tolerate things going right or unable to tolerate success. In the language of Transactional Analysis as explained by Thomas Harris in *I'm O.K.; You're O.K.,* he believes he is Not OK and that other people are OK. His life script or life style is based upon the assumption that he is Not OK. He somehow or other seems committed to validating his Not OK-ness.

Because of his low self-opinion and because very little ever seems to go right, marriage to the Pessimist is difficult. Even if something does go right, he cannot be happy about it as he knows tragedy is soon to follow. He essentially operates upon the premise that: "If things are going so well, can disaster be far behind?" For people suffering from this syndrome, I often suggest they hang a banner in the house which says:

> If things are going so well,
> can disaster be far behind?

Phooey

As we look at the history of the Eternal Pessimist, we find he was conditioned to develop a pessimistic view of life. His developmental years may have been filled with tragedy. As a result of this, he developed the feeling that if he were pessimistic, he would not be disappointed when it rained on his parade. Also, the Eternal Pessimist's parents may have conveyed to him that he was *quite* a disappointment. The comment, "Why can't you be the kind of boy we can be proud of?" rings in his ears. Consistent with his self-fulfilling prophecy, he would then go about disappointing his parents.

The Eternal Pessimist views himself as a second-class citizen. He may have come to realize that his parents preferred another sibling over him. He develops a helpless and hopeless attitude.

The general attitudes of society also lead to the development of this pessimistic view. Many people who are the products of alcoholic parents or broken homes develop the feeling that sooner or later things have to go wrong. They were conditioned to this from childhood as eventually something always went wrong. On the other hand, the larger society has a bias that dictates that the person with alcoholic parents or who comes from a broken family is going to have problems. The prophecy does not have to come true. However, again consistent with the concept of the self-fulfilling prophecy, there is a risk that an individual may internalize this bias and fulfill the prophecy.

I saw an engaged couple who were to be married within a week. The husband-to-be had developed more than the normal case of prenuptial jitters. They came to my attention when the man canceled the wedding plans explaining he was not good enough for his bride-to-be and he did not want to drag her down with him. As we reviewed his life, we discovered he had done well in school, had very rewarding friendships, and had a successful work history. However, he also explained that his father was alcoholic and that his parents divorced when he was in the eighth grade. As a result of the early developmental experiences and of the bias of society, he believed that sooner or later the roof was going to fall in. He did not want his fiancee to have to go down the tube with him.

One woman who had a similar history explained to me that one of her children said, "It's so good to have a mother who had an unhappy family. Because your mother and dad were not nice, you try so hard to be a good mother." In spite of this reassurance from her daughter, the lady continued to believe she was not doing an adequate job as mother.

While in the military, my colleagues and I in the Neuropsychiatric Clinic frequently noticed this phenomenon. As a result of rank, advancement in the military is more overtly evident than in civilian life. We found that many people maintained a spotless military record for several years and were promoted through the ranks at a rate commensurate with their performance. However, we noticed that the Eternal Pessimist attained a certain level and would "goof up royally." This change in behavior from that of an ideal airman or officer to one who could do nothing right demonstrated that he could only tolerate so much success before demonstrating, "Really, I'm Not OK." The same phenomenon, although not as easily identified, is noticed in civilian careers. It is alluded to by Laurence J. Peter in his book, *The Peter Principle,*[2] in which the author suggests that people are promoted until they attain their maximum level of incompetence.

It is certainly true that people have inherent capacities and intelligence and that only a certain level of achievement is possible. However, it is frequently the Not OK feelings rather than one's inherent capacity and intelligence which causes a pattern of successful achievement to be reversed.

The Eternal Pessimist must place his developmental experiences into perspective. He may be like the master rug weaver in the Middle East. Each rug is hand-produced by a crew of men and boys who work under the direction of one master weaver. Since ordinarily they work from the under side of the rug-to-be, it frequently happens that a weaver absent-mindedly makes a mistake and introduces a color that is not according to the pattern. When this occurs, the master weaver, instead of having the work pulled out in order to correct the color sequence, will find some way to incorporate the

---

[2]Laurence J. Peter, *The Peter Principle,* (New York: Morrow, 1969).

mistake harmoniously into the overall pattern. This is a useful object lesson, for we all can learn to take these traumatic experiences from the past and weave them advantageously into a greater pattern of our life.

I have suggested that each of us recognize our emotional sensitivities as well as the sensitivities of our spouse. When we notice that our reactions are too strong, it is necessary to look at our developmental experiences in order to understand the reason for these over-reactions. I have listed various syndromes in order to help couples come to a concrete idea of the various sensitivities shared by many people and the way in which these sensitivities develop.

Some people can use the notion of insight and understanding as an excuse for not changing. For instance, a person may have a habit such as yelling, fighting, over-eating, etc. They may then seek to find the reason that they would have this habit protesting that they want to change and that they need to find the reason they are this way in order to change.

In essence, this search for insight becomes a reason for not changing. Somehow, they never find quite the right explanation for their behavior. Therefore, there is no need to change.

Instead of being so obsessed with the idea of insight, one might be much better off to simply decide to change. At times, it is necessary for one to honestly admit that they are not prepared to or not yet ready to change.

I suggest that it is frustrating to look for permanent and irreversible change in our behavioral reactions or in our personalities. This concept will be discussed more completely in the next chapter.

CHAPTER 5

Adapting To Each Other

In the third chapter, it was suggested that most marital conflicts result from unresolved sensitivities carried from our developmental to our adult life. Also, it was suggested that spouses need to become aware of these sensitivities. This awareness prevents the feelings associated with these sensitivities from avalanching out of control. The fourth chapter discussed various syndromes (sensitivities) and offered possible explanations for the development of these sensitivities. This chapter will examine the particular effect these sensitivities have upon marital interaction. The reader is asked to continue trying to come to grips with who he is, who the other is, and how each spouse became the kind of person he or she is. Since spouses waste valuable time trying to change each other, it is wise to examine ways in which they can adapt to each other rather than to change the other.

It was previously suggested that during developmental years children learn a language of behavior. Although the language generally serves people well, sensitivities develop causing people to over-react to certain stimuli. For some, the developmental experiences were so traumatic that their sensitivities are continually being struck.

For most people, it can be assumed that the developmental experiences have been relatively positive. Therefore, many adults continue to speak the language learned during their developmental years. If the early experiences were pleasant, we may never question the language we learned. In this sense, marriage is like a man from France and a woman from Germany being dropped into a third country. The language each of them brings with them does not permit them to understand each other. It becomes necessary to learn another language-life style. Each spouse is convinced that theirs is the correct life style. Rather than to focus upon adaptation and adjustment to the other, most couples try to get the other spouse to speak their native tongue.

My wife and I became aware of this concept while driving to visit her family. As we neared their home, our four-year-old daughter said, "Let me see, we are going to visit Grandma and Grandpa Lehar. They will shake my hand. It's Grandma and Grandpa Quesnell who kiss me." My wife and I looked at each other, suddenly realizing that Cathy's simple statement explained some of the strain and tension we experienced during our married life. For years, I criticized the life style of her parents thinking they were aloof and austere Germans. On the other hand, my wife thought my family was hysterical. She did not understand why we hugged and kissed each other when we arrived for a visit. She was confused when my dad got the bath towels (to be used for handkerchiefs) when we were ready to leave. We had to come to grips with the realization that each life style was *right,* we had each been exposed to *different* life experiences, and we now needed to find a life style which was acceptable to each of us.

We again realized the different language we learned when we came to buy a home after some ten years of marriage. My father-in-law offered us money to help with the down payment of the home. In my "country," when someone offers to do something unusual, I initially say, "No, that's all right, I can make it." The other person is then supposed to say, "Oh, come on now, we want to help you out." I would then accept the gift. However, speaking different languages, my father-in-law said, "Oh, I'm sorry, we would have liked to have helped you out."

We spend several years learning our particular language-life style. Therefore, adjustment and modification are difficult. As was mentioned in the previous chapter in a time of crisis, we may revert to a language we thought we had forgotten. While I was in grade school, the sisters instructed us to thank them whenever they punished us. They believed their punishment of us would help us gain salvation. It was not until I received a traffic ticket twenty-five years later that I realized how well I learned my lesson. As the patrolman handed me the ticket, I thanked him profusely. His puzzled look suggested to me that he did not know I was grateful to him for helping me gain the perfection that would help me attain salvation.

Most of us do not realize that other people have learned a life style that is different from ours. We go along merrily believing that ours is the right way. Perhaps it is the adjustment to these differences that caused one critic to quip that marriage is a three ring circus: an engagement ring, a wedding ring, and "suffer ring." A couple may agree on major issues of life such as politics, social justice, and religion. During engagement, that couple believes they will have no difficulties in marriage. Unfortunately, this leaves many other issues which the couple must cope with. There is the whole matter of their Frenchness and their Germanness. One may believe that 74° is a comfortable temperature for the home. The other may believe that a temperature of 70° saves a few cents a month and, "What's the difference if you have to wear a wool sweater?" One squeezes the toothpaste from the bottom of the tube and is upset when the other spouse squeezes it in the middle. One spouse may believe Christmas should be celebrated on December 24. However, the other spouse believes the holiday should be celebrated on the 25th. One spouse believes that all birthdays and anniversaries should be celebrated; the other celebrates only the 25th and 50th anniversaries.

These necessary adjustments suggest why marriage is a continual task at which couples must work. It is similar to mixing oil and water. It may mix for a time, but unless there is continued stirring (work), the water and oil will separate. Working at marriage helps prevent separation and alienation. We must remember the tendency to slip back into the earlier language we learned. Also, there is the inclination to interpret different behavior as a sign that our spouse does not love us. Unless we recognize the necessity of, and are willing to make the necessary adjustments, we may be like the man who was out of town and having breakfast in a restaurant. He gave the waitress the following order, "Bring me some warm orange juice, no ice, burn the toast to a crisp, put a couple of sloppy eggs fried in grease on a dirty plate, a cup of coffee that tastes like mud, and be sure to leave the grounds in the cup. Now bring my order just that way and don't change a thing." The waitress complied and said, "Is there anything else I can do for you, Mister?" "Yeah," he grunted, "Now sit down and nag me. I'm homesick!"

Couples involved in interfaith marriages often explain that the theological differences between their religions do not cause them nearly the difficulty as the cultural implications of being German Lutheran and Irish Catholic or Italian Catholic and Southern Baptist.

The preceding comments have suggested that, in a very real sense, we do marry the family of our spouse. Each of us brings into marriage all of the beliefs, attitudes, and ways of living that were intrinsic to our particular family. These influences brought from the family of origin continue to affect the conjugal family. While learning a foreign language, people find they can learn to understand another language before they learn to speak it. In the same vein, it is not necessary that we learn to speak the other person's language, but it is necessary to understand it. With this understanding, a couple can seek to develop a language—life style— which is acceptable to each of them. Again, these adjustments do not come easily. Even if a spouse *wants* to make changes in the earlier life style, he may fear he is being a traitor to his parents. He thinks, "It worked for my mother and dad, it was good for us kids, why isn't it good enough for us?"

It has been intimated that there is no particular language or life style that is objectively right. Unfortunately, in marriage, spouses try to *change* each other rather than to seek to *adjust* to each other. I am impressed with the notion of languages whenever a couple comes to my office explaining, "What we need is a referee," or "What we need is a judge." I explain to them that a marriage counselor can be neither a referee or a judge. We serve more as interpreters. If we seek to be referees, we soon find that the husband is playing football by the American rules and the wife is playing by the Canadian rules. If we seek to be judges, we soon discover one is living by the Anglo-Saxon code of law whereas the other is living by the Hammurabian code of justice. Each is right from his own point of view. This is why it is often hard to understand why many couples should have difficulties in marriage. From what we know of the husband or the wife, each is a fine person. However, marriage is somewhat like mixing two chemicals (such as vinegar and baking powder) which, by themselves, are relatively inactive. However, when they are mixed together, there is a reaction.

In marriage, we need to come to appreciate the individuality and distinctness of our spouse. Clyde Cluckhohn commented, "Every man is in certain respects like all other men, like some other men, and like no other man." A Chinese proverb states it nicely, "We must allow the other to be other." Also, people have frequently commented that couples ought not to "get hitched at the altar if they have the urge to alter." During the course of engagement, couples tend to deny the reality or possible impact of these differences. They may assume that it doesn't make any difference or that "he will change as soon as we are married." It often seems that one marries a person with whom they are in love and who they think is the most wonderful person in the world. It is peculiar that one then tries so hard to change that person shortly after the marriage. In her book, *The Snake Has All The Lines,* Jean Kerr comments, "Marrying a man is like buying something you have been admiring a long time in a shop window. You may love it when you get it home, but it does not always go with everything else in the house." I have suggested that we should not expect these sensitive spots to be alleviated. Dealing with them presents a chronic problem for us. It is the same with adjusting to the different life styles in marriage. It is something at which we must always work and we cannot look for the job to be over and done with once and for all. It is necessary for couples to discuss ways in which they are going to adjust to their differences. However, they should not be discouraged by setbacks. It is less frustrating to expect some of the same old problems to reappear time and time again. After all, some believe that, "history is nothing but the same damn thing happening all over again."

The same is true with the quirks within our personality and within our marriage. Although we continue to run into the same old battles, the same old conflicts, and the same old shortcomings, we need to resolve to try to do better each time. However, when these conflicts and problems continue to be resurrected, we should re-resolve that we will get hold of the problem for the time being. For instance, Shirley had come to recognize that her earlier peer group experiences were the basic cause of the severe discomfort she experienced whenever she and Brad were with other couples. It was difficult for ever-confident Brad to understand why anyone should be afraid of people. Even though Brad and Shirley began to understand the tension and arguing that always developed before any party or social situation, they could not, immediately, eliminate the problem. However, through a series of re-resolutions, they were able to reduce the tension and find a constructive way to deal with these situations. If they had expected insight to immediately eradicate the problem, they would have been disillusioned and scrapped the plan which later became helpful to them.

However, if couples do not have a basic plan for approaching these necessary adaptations, they read various articles and develop a scatter-gun approach to marital adjustment. Their search for *a* magic solution hampers their ability to enrich their relationship. Rather than look for *the one* solution to the painful and uncomfortable adjustments required in marriage, a couple is better advised to view adjustment as a continuing process. This task of marriage is exemplified by the fable in which a peasant is on his death bed and tells his sons that a treasure is buried in the field. After the father's death, the sons dig everywhere in order to discover the treasure. They do not find it, but their labor improves the soil and secures for them a good living. The treasure in the fable symbolizes married life. Happiness does not come from the deliberate search for the *one* answer designed to solve all problems. However, in continuing our search—in laboring to discover each other—couples may find the state of well-being which can emanate from marriage.

Basically couples need to identify when they should struggle and when they should wait for the anxiety to pass. A spouse is like the swimmer who suddenly finds himself caught in a whirlpool. Each year, many people drown because they do not know how to swim once they are caught in a swirling pool of water. No one needs to drown in a whirlpool if he will only wait a moment and hold his breath. Just as the water pulls him down, so, in a few seconds, it also spills him out again. The drownings occur whenever a person tries to help himself against the current. The struggle exhausts him and he drowns.

It is much the same with our emotional life. Sometimes we should just hold our breath and wait for the crisis to pass. The secret of life is to know when to keep trying and when to ride the whirlpool. The wisdom of life is found in the prayer of Alcoholics Anonymous:

> God, give me the serenity
> to accept what I cannot change,
> the courage to change what I can,
> and the wisdom to know the difference.

The next chapter will describe the way in which various personalities fit together in marriage.

CHAPTER 6

Who Am I?

This is a continuation of the theme of the previous chapter which stressed the importance of appreciating interpersonal differences and of finding ways to adjust to these differences rather than to try to change the other. However, it is important to stress that spouses can sometimes use the adjustment concept as a "cop out." That is, one might say, "This is who I am and you can't expect me to change." As much as it is necessary to adjust to each other, it is also important to understand what it is like to live with someone with our personality. If we ask the other person to accept us as we are, we must understand whether or not our expectations are unrealistic.

This chapter will identify and discuss some various types of personalities. The reader is asked to identify whether or not one or more of the descriptions fits him. If it does, he should consider what it is like to live with somebody like him.

The Double-Binder

The double-binder is the spouse who frequently places his mate in the position of being damned if he does and damned if he doesn't. A husband may go to work in the morning leaving his wife with a list of jobs including shopping for a birthday present for his mother, getting the power lawn mower repaired, and the car to the garage. He may have also given her a list of several people she is to call. He may come home at night and be upset that the house is messy and that he isn't having a gourmet dinner. We need to look at ourselves in order to see if we have expectations of our spouse which continually place him in the position of disappointing us in one area while trying to please us in another. Dan Greenburg[1] describes the double-bind explaining that the Jewish mother ironed two shirts for her son. The shirts were hanging in his room and he decided to wear one. When he came downstairs, his mother looked at him, saw the shirt, and said, "Oh, you didn't like the other shirt I ironed for you." The squeeze was experienced by the man who cooked breakfast for his wife on Mother's Day. He asked her what she would like and she explained that she wanted two eggs. He then asked, "How do you want the eggs?" She replied, "One fried and one scrambled." The husband worked on the eggs, not wanting the fried one to be runny or hard and wanting the scrambled egg to be fluffy and yellow. He proudly placed the eggs before his wife asking, "How's that, dear?" She replied, "You fried the wrong one."

Mary Martyr and Holy Joe

As one studies the history of the saints, two interesting phenomena are discovered. One is that most saints were members of religious orders. From this, one can conclude either that secular clergy do not lead as saintly lives as do members of orders or that members of religious orders take the time to work for the canonization of their departed

---

[1]Dan Greenburg, *How To Be A Jewish Mother,* (Los Angeles, California: Price, Stern, Sloan, Inc., 1964), p. 16.

brothers and sisters. The other phenomenon which is noted is that very few saints are married. Again, there are two interpretations. One might conclude that married life is not conducive to sanctity or one might conclude that no one can tolerate being married to a saint. I rather prefer the latter explanation.

It is difficult to be married to a saint. Also, it is embarrassing to live with the idea that one is so imperfect that it is only the special grace with which one's spouse is endowed that permits him or her to tolerate the marriage. The other's saintliness magnifies one's own imperfections. The halo is frequently used to strangle the "unholy spouse." The Mary Martyr syndrome is easy to identify in the waiting room. Mary Martyr sits with her head slightly tilted. Her eyes are cast both downward to punctuate her humility and upward to stress her saintliness. The nonverbal message seems to be, "Dear God, thank you for giving me the grace to contend with this burden (my spouse) that you have placed upon my shoulders. I only regret that I have but one circulatory system to bleed upon the altar of sacrifice for my family."

Holy Joe once went to his doctor complaining of headaches. He explained that he could not understand why he should have headaches as he didn't drink, stay up late, or chase women. The doctor looked at him and said, "Perhaps your halo is on too tight." One wife complained she was bored just sitting around the house all the time. Holy Joe explained he could certainly understand her boredom. He left for work at 6:30 A.M., returned about 4:00, had a quick lunch, left for his second job, and did not return from his second job until about 11:00 or 12:00. He understood there wasn't much for his wife to do but sit around and take care of the house. He explained, "Just because I have to work so hard to put bread on the table and to clothe the kids is no reason that she should have to suffer." With that kind of understanding from her husband, the wife could hardly justify being unhappy with her own situation.

Neddy Neat (Nadine) and Mr. Perfect
vs.
Messy Morris (Maureen)

We might look closely at ourselves and find that we fall into the category of Neddy Neat. Neddy has a need for everything to be in order believing that, "There is a place for everything and everything must be in its place." He comments that, "A cluttered desk is a sign of a cluttered mind." He never bothers to say what an empty desk is a sign of.

At any rate, everything must be in order. There is total panic if somebody should dirty the ashtrays in the car or walk through the house with dirty shoes. Nadine Neat scrubs and waxes the kitchen floor in the midst of the holiday dinner. Her living room furniture is upholstered in offwhite— i.e., all the furniture is covered with sheets so the upholstery will not get dirty. She believes that front doors are only for decorative effect and everyone should use the back door.

I was once having lunch with Neddy Neat. We were eating in a restaurant in which customers are to throw peanut shells and cigarette ashes on the floor. I threw shells on the floor, but when I glanced at my companion who had a fist full of peanut shells, he exclaimed, "I can't, I can't mess up the floor."

As much as life with Neddy or Nadine becomes trying, it is no less difficult to live with Messy Morris or Maureen who panics at cleaning time. Morris does not believe in disturbing the ecology of his environment. The popular TV program, *The Odd Couple,* exemplifies the difficulties a Neddy Neat and Messy Maureen would have in marriage.

Mr. Perfect is my favorite person. Except for the way he picks at people, he is very similar to Neddy and Nadine. His family asks, "Does he always have to pick, pick, pick?" His garage is neat and all the tools are carefully hung in a special place. God help the person who gets into his tools. It may take him a long time to complete a task, but when completed, he is well satisfied with his masterpiece. There is not a dandelion in his yard, the car is carefully waxed and polished, and it looks as if it never snows in his driveway.

My affinity for Mr. Perfect resulted from one of our family camping trips. (By the way, I believe that the family that camps together deserves what they get.) On one of our trips, I went through the usual ritual of cajoling the children to get them to help. If they were not pitching in, I would declare, "This is our last camping trip!" Their eyes would be cast heavenward as they prayed to God that this, indeed, might be the last trip. At any rate, we went fishing. While coming into shore, I faced the momentous decision whether we would tie the boat to the dock or leave it on shore. I decided to run in onto the shore, but as we passed the dock, I changed my mind, grabbed the dock, and knocked our older son into the water. After Mike calmed down, our younger son looked up at me and exclaimed, "Mista Poifect goofed!" Now they keep a weekly count of "Mista Poifect's goofs."

Nervous Nellie or Ned the Worrier
vs.
Happy Harry (Harriet)

Nellie and Ned preface their statements by asking, "Is this a problem? Should I worry about that?" It is as though there were an obligation to be nervous and upset. They have callouses on their fingers from pushing the panic button. Nellie and Ned need to realize that it is all right not to worry and that life can be lived spontaneously. Again, these personality factors are the cause of greater tension if the couples operate at opposite ends of a continuum. That is, Nellie and Ned's agreement to panic makes for a compatible relationship. On the other hand, a marriage between Ned and Happy Harriet would be trying. Harriet sees no cause for concern believing it is foolish to get shook over anything as all will turn out all right in the end. Harry & Harriet live in a continual state of euphoria believing that all problems can be brushed aside with a good joke or a quick bit of laughter. They see no sense in worrying about something today when one can wait until tomorrow to worry.

By and large, Harry and Harriet are nice to be around, but it is trying when they refuse to take anything seriously or when they pull one practical joke after the other. Harry and Harriet irresponsibly put off jobs until tomorrow.

Silent Sam
vs.
Gabby Abby

Silent Sam believes that silence is a virtue. He contends that one should speak softly and carry a big stick. He believes that, "People who talk are like leaky pitchers—everything runs out of them;" or "Great talkers are great liars." He also believes that, "It is better to remain silent and be thought dumb than to speak and remove all doubt." He has little sympathy for the view of Benjamin Franklin who believed that, "The big man who does things makes many mistakes, but he never makes the biggest mistake of all, doing nothing." Sam's wife never really knows what he is thinking since he believes silence is a virtue.

On the other hand, Gabby Abby abhors any vacuum in conversation. She believes it necessary to keep her jaws moving all the time. It is difficult for anyone to interupt her.

She is never at a loss for words and has no trouble tying up the telephone most of the day. One may never know for certain what she is saying, but she does manage to keep things going. When Abby calls her friends, they listen for a few minutes, set down the receiver, and go about their work picking up the phone every few minutes to utter a few "uh huhs."

The Myth That Opposites Attract

We frequently hear the comment that opposites attract each other. The idea is that people of two distinctly different personalities can correct for each other and thereby find a middle ground. This may be true for very mature people who are convinced that there are alternative life styles. However, it is very difficult for people of distinctly different personalities to adjust to each other. Several studies of marital satisfaction conclude that the more alike couples are, the easier it is for them to adjust to each other in marriage.

Differences in personality do, indeed, attract men and women to each other. These differences precipitate a love reaction and the couple enters into marriage. For instance, a shy and withdrawn man may be attracted to an extroverted woman. The happy couple decide to marry and their friends are ecstatic. The friends comment, "Don is so different since meeting Marge. She has taught him how to have fun and enjoy life." On the other hand, other friends comment that, "Marge is so much more calm now that she has met Don. She was so excitable and always had to be on the go. Don is such a calming and soothing influence." It is generally agreed that this will be a wonderful union. The couple enter into marriage and are quite satisfied for the first several months. Then, the impact of the personality differences hits full force. Suddenly, one Saturday evening, Marge tires of watching TV. She suggests they go out. Don asks, "Marge, don't you love me? Why do we have to go out? Isn't it enough to just sit here and be with each other?" Marge asks, "Don, don't you love me? Are you ashamed to be out in public with me? Don't you want to do some of the things that I enjoy?" Although the impact of these differences is initially unrecognized or denied, the couple must effectively come to grips with the reality of these differences and effect a meaningful adaptation to each other. If they fail to make these adaptations, feelings of alienation rather than affiliation will destroy the relationship. Voltaire explains, "You always get what you want out of life, but you do not always know what you want until you get it, which keeps us so dissatisfied." In this example, Don and Marge may realize they really desired someone with a similar personality.

The couple who agrees to be up by 6:15 every morning, have breakfast at 6:43, have the husband leave for work at 6:59, arrive home at 4:58, and begin eating evening dinner at 5:28 easily adjusts to each other. Another husband may follow this schedule, but his wife may believe it is unnecessary to get up before noon, see no need to wash the dishes when they will only be dirtied six hours later, and see no need to clean the house when it will be messed up when the kids get home. This couple *may* experience some difficulties adjusting to each other.

In some marriages, the husband places a low priority upon the role of homemaker. He may not enjoy puttering around the home and place more emphasis upon enjoying himself away from the home. In general, he does not place high priority upon home and hearth. He may pressure his wife to go out of the home to work. In doing this, he belittles what she does at home with the children and belittles her efforts to create a comfortable home life. If his wife places high value upon her role as homemaker, she will resent his lack of appreciation of her efforts and resent the pressure he applies to get her to work outside of the home. If the couple places equal value upon home and hearth, the adjustment to marriage is less traumatic.

A similar adjustment problem is experienced with the Public Health Department syndrome as compared with the Emergency Room syndrome. A spouse with a Public Health Department syndrome plans for the future. He is a good scout whose motto is: "Be prepared." He would not think of spending any money until there were several thousand dollars in the savings account. On the other hand, the Emergency-Roomer doesn't concern himself with the future believing he is well equipped to handle any eventuality. He does whatever he can at the present time anticipating he will be able to deal with whatever emergencies arise.

Perhaps the type of adjustment required of couples is exemplified by the marriage between the Jewish man and the Christian woman. Their friends wondered how they would celebrate Christmas. They solved this problem by having a Christmas tree and topping it with the Star of David.

In many situations, couples seek to change each other in a subtle fashion. Rather than bring their differences out into the open and discuss alternative ways of adjustment, they subtly seek to get the other to come around to their way of thinking. The thought is, of course, that this will help them grow in affiliation. The eventual result is that the couple becomes more alienated. This can be exemplified by taking a personality trait such as volatility and placing it on a scale from zero to ten. Zero indicates that the person is extremely passive and ten suggests extreme volatility. If a husband has a rating of "6" on the volatility scale and his wife has a rating of "4," we might find the husband talking to himself in this way, "It really is nice living with Judy. She's calm and doesn't get excited. On the other hand, I don't always know where she stands and I wish she would be more expressive. In order to draw her out a bit more, I am going to accelerate myself to a "7." In that way, she will come up to a "5," we won't be so far apart, and I will know where she stands." However, while Bob is saying this, Judy is saying, "By and large, it's nice to live with Bob. I know where he stands on all issues. However, in some instances he gets too excited. I wish he would be more calm. In order to effect this, I think I will decelerate to a "3," that will reduce him to a "5," he won't be quite so excitable, and we will be closer together.

As one can see, the intention of Bob and Judy was to subtly effect a change in the other that would draw them closer together. Unfortunately, the eventual result was further alienation. This phenomenon is frequently noticed when two people are talking with each other. If one speaks in a loud voice and the other in a soft voice, they try to correct for each other. The one with the louder voice talks louder in order to get the softer voiced individual to speak more loudly. While this is going on, the person with the softer voice talks more softly so the person with the louder voice will tone down. Within a few minutes, the one is screaming and the other is whispering.

It is generally risky for couples to focus just upon what they want the other person to change without realizing what that individual may want them to change in themselves. For instance, one couple read an article in which they were advised to write down the things that they did not like about the other. The husband wrote that he wished his wife would stop smoking and that she would lose weight. As he read his wife's list, he found she had written that she wished he would stop complaining about her weight and her smoking. In marriage, spouses should recognize their propensity for, and the dangers of, spending most of their time looking for ways and means of supporting their own way of living. Adjustment to each other, rather than changing each other, must have a higher priority. However, some couples make their antagonistic differences sound complementary as did one wife who explained to a marriage counselor that she and her husband had the same interests, "He likes to save money and I like to spend it."

Couples must learn to recognize, to talk about, to tolerate, and to understand their interpersonal differences. It is a sad fact that in many marriages there are certain subjects which are never discussed. There are senseless little islands of secrecy which serve no purpose except to perpetuate the hidden rancors and subtle hostilities. A discussion of these special problems turns inevitably into violent arguments and mutual recriminations. Often, in a sort of self-defiance, the couple agree, either tacitly or verbally, to avoid the subject entirely. Silence, however, does not solve the problem. It merely buries it. The two become uneasy because they cannot discuss these troublesome areas. Mistrust of each other builds added ill will and the gap widens.

I have seen several bizarre efforts on the part of spouses to change each other. However, perhaps the most bizarre occurred when a "Mr. Perfect" appeared at my office explaining that he had finally found the girl he intended to marry. He literally searched throughout the world to find her. He explained that she was attractive, intelligent, and sociable. However, he mentioned she had one little flaw—she had too much of a mind of her own and he wanted that changed.

In seeking to change the other, we may find ourselves in the position of the husband who explained that he wanted his wife to be a lady in the parlor, an economist in the kitchen, and a hussy in the bedroom. Sometime after marriage, a friend asked him how things had turned out. He explained that everything was reversed. "She is a hussy in the parlor, a lady in the kitchen, and an economist in the bedroom."

Couples need not feel guilty because they cannot agree on everything. Each must try to see the other as a unique human being, the partner with whom they have chosen to work out their eternal salvation. They must seek to discover and understand the nature of their differences and to live with them more easily. Carl R. Rogers, the famous psychologist, explains that, "People are just as wonderful as sunsets if I can let them be. I don't try to control a sunset. I watch it with awe as it unfolds and I like myself best when appreciating the unfolding of a life." We can change ourselves, but it is generally damaging to the relationship to try to change our spouse.

Each of the partners involved in a Christian marriage has a serious obligation to use every means, spiritual and psychological, to help himself achieve individual emotional maturity. Only in this way can a man or woman bring to the marriage state a healthy self-love and a self-respect, which, in turn, generates a true, lasting and mature love and respect for one's partner. Emotional maturity coupled with natural love and blessed by God—the author of all life and love—is the foundation stone for a healthy, happy, holy marriage.

BIBLIOGRAPHY

Berne, Eric. *Games People Play*. New York: Grove Press, 1964.

> Dr. Berne wittily christens and lucidly explains twenty of the games which people jump, fall, or get pushed into. He provides the tried and proven, intellectually elegant antigame with which to liberate yourself from each game whenever you say so.

Bird, Joseph, and Bird, Lois. *Marriage Is For Grownups*. Garden City, New York: Doubleday and Co., 1969.

> A candid analysis of the problem areas which confront every married couple and a discussion of mature, rational ways to work toward their solutions.

Blanck, Rubin, and Blanck, Gertrude. *Marriage and Personal Development*. New York: Columbia University Press, 1968.

> The authors have found that the difficulties between marriage partners can best be understood when seen as reflecting gaps and failures in development.

Greenburg, Dan. *How To Be A Jewish Mother*. Los Angeles, California: Pierce, Stern, Sloan Publishers, Inc., 1964.

> A humorous book which provides a detailed account of how to be a Jewish mother.

Harris, Thomas A. *I'm OK—You're OK: A Practical Guide To Transactional Analysis*. New York: Harper and Row, Publishers, 1969.

Here is a fresh, sensible, increasingly popular approach to the problems that every human being, including the person in need of psychiatric help, faces every day in his relations with himself and others.

Powell, John. *Why Am I Afraid To Tell You Who I Am.* Chicago: Argus Communications, Inc., 1969.

Section III

DISCOVERING THE OTHER

CHAPTER 7

Understanding — Knowing — Loving

Communication is a popular subject for seminars, workshops, and Sunday homilies. Business executives encourage their employees to understand them, clergy prod the members of their parishes and congregations to talk with each other, and wives want husbands to talk with (and listen to) them. This obsession with communication prompted Eric Berne to comment, "Communication is what people talk about when they are having trouble talking." In many situations, communication becomes reduced to a technology rather than to an art. Husbands and wives frequently complain, "He (she) doesn't understand me." This generally means that the one spouse does not think as the other spouse wants him to think. Spouses may complain, "She doesn't talk to me anymore," "He hasn't kissed me in a year"; or as one frustrated woman lamented, "My husband doesn't commute with me anymore!"

The purpose of this section is not to discuss a technology of communication which permits spouses to manipulate each other, but to discuss a philosophy of communication which is based upon the premise that a knowledge of each other leads to an understanding of each other. This understanding of each other leads to the development of a loving relationship. However, consistent with the theme of this book, spouses must *work* at developing effective communication within their marriage. It can only be established when there is a true commitment to and a realization of the covenant and sacramental nature of marriage. Spouses may look for help from the Lord and find themselves feeling like the pastor who insisted that the Good Lord told him what to say each Sunday morning. However, he added, "The sermon still requires several hours of polishing to get it exactly the way He wants it." Only conscientious commitment to the value of effective communication enables spouses to develop the understanding and knowledge of each other which creates the jewel of satisfaction discussed in the first chapter. The concept that love-generating communication does not come easily and spontaneously is exemplified by the lecturer who arrived at the University of Chicago. Since he was about an hour early, he was unconcerned that no one was present to meet him. However, as it got closer to 10:00 A.M., he became increasingly concerned. Finally, he called his secretary to see if she knew what was wrong. She explained, "Doctor, you have the right day and the right time, but the wrong place. You are to be at the University of Iowa and not the University of Chicago." The title of his intended lecture was, "Communication in The Technological Age."

It seems that in many marriages, the spouses are like two strangers who meet on a train. Many have had the experience of being seated next to a person, not saying a word to each other or in any other way validating the existence of the other person. They arrive at their destination as unfamiliar with each other as when they first got into their seats. On the other hand, many have also had the experience of taking advantage of the opportunity to comment about the weather or other small talk ways of introducing conversation. This leads to the development of a pleasant transitory relationship. In fact, many actual friendships develop from conversations like that just described.

John Powell explains that Jesus struggled a lifetime to say what was inside himself. He, too, learned a language. He was taught to speak, corrected in his errors, encouraged when He got it right. Slowly, painfully, the mystery of the human word took root in his life. He who would one day speak the Beatitudes put his first sentences together ungrammatically. This Jesus, whose human words would awesomely reveal God, once stammered as did we. He blushed at his mistakes and flushed with success when he overcame them. This statement suggests the work involved in developing effective communication.

Unfortunately, as we will discuss later, spouses frequently believe that talk is something reserved for the resolution of problems. When one asks a husband if he has talked with his wife in the past few days, the husband may become very nervous and ask, "Why? What's wrong?" The idea is that you talk with each other when there is a problem. This is exemplified by the two men who developed the habit of stopping at a small coffee shop before starting home from work. For several months, they had taken the same counter seats each evening at 5:20 with neither of them ever speaking a word to each other. One evening, one of the men was late. As the other man was paying the cashier on his way out, the tardy gentleman entered, walked up to the man paying his bill, and said, "I'm sorry I'm so late. Believe me, I was tied up in a meeting until now!" Not a word had been exchanged between the two of them until there was a problem.

The problems of nonunderstanding and noncommunication are so great between spouses that we must make the best use of language in our efforts to deal effectively with our marital relationship. It will become apparent throughout this section that we *cannot not* communicate. Talking is only one of the ways in which we communicate. If we do not talk with each other, we are communicating. The only problem is that we may not know for certain what it is we are communicating.

Spouses use talking-type communication in order to solve various problems and conflicts, make decisions, and to relieve tension and unburden the mind. Most importantly, talking-type communication enables the couple to develop the understanding and awareness that enables them to nurture their love relationship. It is the transmission of feelings, attitudes, facts, beliefs, and ideas between spouses. It is a way in which we seek to influence and understand one another as one man quipped:

> A long life is barely enough for a man
> and a woman to understand each other, and
> to be understood is to love. The man who
> understands a woman is qualified to
> understand pretty well everything.

> (Author Unknown)

One of the greatest gifts God has given to spouses is the power to give life to one another. Through the medium of speech, spouses can communicate or destroy life in one another.

We realize that some people simply do not understand the importance of talking with each other. Within their family of origin, the parents may have made all of the decisions. Therefore, they may not have become accustomed to talking things out. Because of that, a spouse may not really know how to talk with the other or may fail to see the importance of talking-type communication. Spouses frequently comment, "I know what she is thinking and what she wants so why spend time talking about it." These spouses fail to see the value in sharing one's hopes, dreams, and hurts. Also, many spouses fear being hurt by the other. As a result of this, they decide that the best way to avoid pain is to keep quiet. They may have experienced pain and injury earlier in the marriage and decided that "silence is the best policy."

It is necessary to recognize that effective communication is a dialogue. It is a "reciprocal relationship in which each party 'experiences the other side' so that their communication becomes a true address and response in which each informs and learns. . . . It is distinct from monologue."[1] In some relationships, the dialogue seems more like two opposing sides hollering at each other through bull horns. It is only the extremist who thinks communication means agreeing with him.

The development of meaningful marital dialogue depends upon commitment to the belief that there is something to know about the other person and that he has something important to offer. It is based upon a four-pronged system of communication. This is a system in which there is a message sent, a message is received, that message is checked out and sent back, and the "checkout" is received by the initiator and confirmed as accurate, or corrected and modified.

Messages must be sent, received, and checked out. In many marriages, the communication is more like two fans blowing at each other. Instead of listening, the spouses talk at each other. Man's mind is like a parachute: to work, it first has to be open. Our minds must be open to the other. We need to develop the art of listening. If one recognizes that the hardest thing in the world to open is a closed mind, he may also recognize the commensurate need to develop the art of listening. A class in music appreciation was asked the difference between listening and hearing. At first there was no response. Finally, a hand went up and a youngster offered this sage solution, "Listening is wanting to hear." It is neces-

---

[1]Reuel L. Howe, *The Miracle of Dialogue,* (New York: Seabury Press, 1963), p. 50.

sary that we want to hear the other person. Frequently, in marriage, there is the danger that conversation will become a game that is played with pruning shears in which each spouse cuts off the voice of the other as soon as it sprouts. Thomas Merton explained that listening was obsolete. So was silence. He believed that many people were traveling alone in a small blue capsule of indignation. The following poem exemplifies the importance of listening:

> Until a man has learned to listen,
> he has no business teaching;
> until he realizes that every man
> has something of truth and wisdom to offer,
> he does not begin to learn.
> It is only when he sees
> how each of his fellows surpasses him
> that a man begins to be wise
> to himself and to his fellow men.

> (Author Unknown)

Edmund Leach explained that, "Many people have come to feel they live in a world in which they cannot hear anything because everyone is talking at once." The two words "information" and "communication" are often used interchangeably. However, they signify quite different things. Information is giving out; communication is getting through. The four-pronged system described here enables husbands and wives to get through to each other.

In marriage, it is necessary to realize that each person is a special sound. It is important that spouses learn how to listen to each other. In listening, we are able to follow the advice of St. Augustine who has said,

> Let us, you and I, lay aside all arrogance.
> Let neither of us pretend to have found the truth.

Let us seek it as something unknown to both of us.
Then we may seek it with love and sincerity.
    when neither of us has the rashness nor
    presumption to believe that he already
    possesses it.
And if I am asking too much of you,
    allow me to listen to you at least,
    to talk with you as I do with things whom,
    for my part,
    I do not pretend to understand.[2]

Girzaitis continues to stress listening explaining that people need to develop a specific competence—that of Response Ability. She believes that people play games of nonlistening. In this game, people have push-button mechanisms in which they turn off one another. She believes that people are defensive in their communication and that people debate instead of entering into dialogue. She mentions that once, after a homily, a mother told her that her son had said, "I don't want to listen." During the homily, Girzaitis stressed that if people listened, inevitably they would change because they would admit into their minds ideas that had not been there before. She encourages listening with one's heart so as to step inside another's skin. So as to step inside another's skin, walk in his shoes, and attempt to see things from another's point of view. She encourages drawing the other out and to help the significant other feel that we understand he is important.

During the course of weekend renewals, I encourage couples to maintain silence and to walk around the area. I ask them to listen to what is happening. They are instructed to listen to the environment around them and to listen to the

---

[2]Loretta Girzaitis, *Listening—A Response Ability,* (Winona, Minnesota: St. Mary's College Press, 1972), p. 1 (Original reference not given.)

expression of others. They are asked to absorb all that they see. After the listening experience, the couples talk with each other about their quiet experience and the experience of listening to the environment. I then encourage them to talk with each other about the way in which they listen in their marriage. Listening helps couples understand how much more they can learn about the other.

Also, in many marriages, there is a failure to understand the message that is sent. This third stage of checking out the message is conveyed in the following ditty:

> I know that
> You believe you
> Understand what
> You think I said,
>   But
> I am not sure
> You realize that
> What you heard
> Is not
> What I meant.

> (Author Unknown)

The third and fourth stages of checking out and validating or clarifying demonstrates the importance of realizing that the message sent is not always the one received by the spouse. David Knox[3] explains that, "Questions asked by the respective partners which assist them in understanding the meaning of communication include: 'Do you mean. . .?' 'What exactly do you mean?' and 'What does *that* refer to?' Hence the message sent is brought into line with the message received."

---

[3]David Knox, *Marriage Happiness,* (Champaign, Illinois: Research Press Company, 1972), pp. 53-55.

Knox also explains that C. H. Madsen[4] developed the concept that honest, dishonest, direct, and indirect questions were the four critical issues of marital counseling. An honest question is one to which the respondent can respond negatively without penalty. If the husband asks his wife an honest question, he will not get angry at her response. In effect, he wants to know what his wife thinks. The husband who asks his wife, "Do you mind if we spend Christmas with my parents?" is asking her an honest question if she can say "No," without his becoming angry.

A dishonest question is one in which the respondent cannot respond negatively without penalty. If the husband becomes angered when his wife responds, "No, I would not like to spend Christmas with your parents," a dishonest question has been asked. Spouses are assisted in asking honest questions by:

1. Deciding if their questions are honest, and
2. Asking the mate if he is asking an honest question.

The wife who is asked by her husband, "Do you want to visit my parents?" should verify her husband's honesty. Honest questions are important since they keep the partners communicating in a candid way with each other, while dishonest questions make it clear who has the problem.

> Asking a direct question is as important as asking an honest question. A direct question asks specifically what you want to know. "Do you want to have intercourse?" is a direct question whereas, "Are you tired tonight?" is an indirect question if intercourse is desired. Wives sometimes ask their husbands, "How do you like my new dress?" (Indirect question) when they may want to know how appealing they look. . . Hence, direct questions ask for specific information desired and indirect questions

---

[4]C. H. Madsen, Jr., Florida State University, Personal Communications, 1968, 1969, 1970. (Further biographical information not provided by Knox.)

are a subtle way of ascertaining the information which could be
obtained by direct questions.[5]

Knox[6] also provides a very helpful diagram which demonstrates that honest questions are always direct questions. On
the other hand, dishonest questions may be direct or indirect.
Direct questions may be honest or dishonest, whereas indirect questions are always dishonest. Effective communication requires that questions be both honest and direct.

	HONEST	DISHONEST
DIRECT	Excellent Communication	Inadequate Communication
INDIRECT		Inadequate Communication

Couples should seek to develop a system of communication which permits them to grow in understanding, awareness, and love of each other. They should believe that they
and the other are significant, that each has something to say,

[5]Knox, *op. cit.* p. 54.
[6]*Ibid.* p. 55.

and something to be heard. Husbands and wives should also be willing to stick to the task of developing creative communication. The remaining chapters of this section will discuss ways in which couples can capitalize on the potential inherent within each spouse to become an effective communicator.

CHAPTER 8

Be Nice To Each Other: Supportive Communication

The Apostle Paul advises us to "Be kind to one another, compassionate, and mutually forgiving. . ." (Ephesians 4:32). Since spouses frequently overlook the supportive function of communication, Paul's statement is apropos to marriage. Instead of emotionally supporting each other, it appears there is a cultural bias mitigating against accentuating the positive and complimenting one's spouse. The normal and average human being has a definite need for recognition, support, and encouragement. Everybody has to be somebody to be anybody. Yet, there is a prejudice rampant in our society suggesting that one is only to be complimented when he does something outstanding. We can see immediately that this establishes a state of tension. As normal and average human beings, we are not going to do much that is outstanding. In spite of our need for compliments, the sentiment of our society dictates that one cannot be complimented for simply doing his job. Because of this predilection, most spouses go for several years without validation of their existence. This supportive phase of the marital relationship is often neglected. It is similar to the story of the pastor who delivered lengthy homilies. On one Sunday, his assistant stole the last page of his notes. The pastor was preaching in ringing tones and exclaimed, "Adam said to Eve. . ." He turned to what he thought would be the last page of his notes only to find it

96

missing. He lost his composure, stumbled around wondering what to say, and finally exclaimed, "There seems to be a leaf missing!" The supportive and complimentary function is the leaf that is often left out in the marital relationship.

Both in counseling and family life enrichment seminars, I direct the group's attention to several facets of family life. The focus which elicits the most resistance from the group is the discussion of the supportive function in marriage. Many participants rebel against the idea of complimenting each other for simply being normal and doing average, zilchy tasks. One husband angrily exclaimed, "The greatest compliment I pay my wife is to take her for granted." One of the sad facts of modern married life is that we have come to a point of taking our spouse for granted. When one is taken for granted, he begins to feel the other doesn't care. Rather than to operate upon the premise of, "Never say anything unless you have something good to say," we tend to, "Not say anything unless there is something bad to say." We fail to heed Christ's advice not to concern ourselves with the splinter in another man's eye until we have removed the beam from our own. (Luke 6:41)

Because of our society's preoccupation with conflict, we are more geared toward criticism and alienation than we are toward supporting, complimenting, and developing affiliation. We have placed more emphasis upon knowing how to disagree and fight than we have upon learning how to cooperate and be nice to each other.

If we ask any decent person what he thinks matters most in human conduct, his answer may be "human kindness." Yet, we generally fail to take cognizance of this concept in marriage finding it easier to be critical. We tend to zero in upon the inadequacies rather than the adequacies of our spouse. For many insecure people who operate from a "Not OK position," it is necessary to focus upon inadequacies in order to salvage some sense of self-worth. We reinforce our own sense of esteem by zeroing in upon the inadequacies of others. We may gain a feeling of adequacy by determining that others are inadequate. Our attitude is like that of the family returning from church. The father criticized the sermon, the mother thought the organist made several mistakes, and the daughter disliked the choir's singing. However, it was suddenly quiet when little Bill remarked, "I thought that it was a pretty good show . . . for a nickel."

When spouses are encouraged to accentuate the positive, their usual retort is, "I would be happy to compliment him if only he would give me something to compliment him about." Most spouses want their mate to be abnormal. That is, many refuse to accept normality and will only compliment when the spouse manifests superior behavior.

What does someone become if we take him for granted? It may be true, as Shakespeare says, "All the world is a stage." However, within many marriages, it seems that each spouse wants to occupy the critic's seat. We forget that man does not live by bread alone. Every now and then, he needs buttering up. Everyone has his own little claim to some minor distinction. All of us need to feel there is something unique and special about us. We want others to realize our uniqueness and to appreciate that we happen only once in all eternity. We want it known that we have a right to cherish our specialness.

Marriage requires the support exemplified by the man who placed this bumper sticker on the car driven by his wife: "Please don't hit Norma, I love her." Because of the impersonal nature of the larger society, it becomes even more important that spouses be able to look to the marital relationship for support, encouragement, and validation of their worth. A commentator on the CBS radio network related the story of Agnes O'Brien. He explained that she was about seventy years old. When she died, no relatives claimed her remains. She was placed in a plain pine box in the morgue. Her name was typed on a card and tacked to the box. At about 8:00 A.M., a large gray truck drove up to the morgue and loaded her box and thirteen others onto the truck. The loading did not take very long as they did not have to be careful. After all, these boxes did not contain liquor, furniture, glass, or anything very precious. They only contained the remains of Agnes O'Brien and others like her. Who really cared? The truck pulled away from the morgue heading out into the traffic. It passed and was passed by many other vehicles. No one really noticed or paid attention to the gray van as no one had ever really noticed or paid any attention to Agnes O'Brien. Somewhere in the past or in the very distant past, there must have been someone who knew Agnes, there must have been somebody who cared, there must have been someone to whom she was important, but now she was of no importance. The van moved along stopping at a second morgue where twenty more pine boxes were quickly loaded. They continued along in the New York traffic finally coming to the burying grounds.

At this point, there was a group of prisoners who were assigned to the burial detail. There was a large trench about three feet deep and the boxes were laid side by side. You could still see the boxes from the previous day as they had not yet been completely covered by the earth. One of the prisoners took a large marking pen and wrote Agnes' name in large letters across the top of the box. That was perhaps the largest her name had ever been written. The box was then placed into the ground and its exact location carefully noted in official records. The soil in the burying grounds had a high concentration of lime and in about twenty-five years all of the remains of Agnes O'Brien would turn to compost and no one would ever know she had lived.

In the same vein, a dentist in an office next to ours recently retired after some forty years of practice. I stopped by to see him on his last day as he was packing his records and equipment. I was overwhelmed by the loneliness of this man who was simply "putting it all away." He had reached the end of his career and he was exiting by himself. I was overwhelmed by the sadness of the situation as I realized that none of us had become aware of his pending retirement and we had in no way bothered to arrange for a coffee or some recognition of the services he had offered to the community.

Husbands often comment that no one needs to thank them for doing their job. If a husband is a mechanic, he explains that if somebody brings in their car for repairs and is able to drive their car away from the shop, he knows he has done his job and he needs no thanks. In the same way, his wife is simply supposed to do her job, unrewarded by any special recognition. However, a man needs to recognize that he works in a world which is quite different from that of his wife. At the end of a day, he can generally look about and see what he has done. For his wife, it is a different story. She gets the children off to school, goes grocery shopping, selects a gift for the anniversary of her husband's parents, and then cleans the house. Along about mid-afternoon, it looks as though the tornado actually missed their house and everything seems to be in order. Just as the mother is breathing a sigh of relief, the children come home from school. Within a few minutes, it looks as though the tornado struck again. The husband comes home a couple hours later, surveys the disaster area, and exclaims, "What's wrong around this house! Have you been talking to your sister on the phone all day?"

Frequently, husbands undermine the importance of the homemaking vocation. They perceive it as something anyone can do and attach low status to the position. If a husband attaches low status to one of his wife's life vocations, she begins to feel unimportant. The wife of a surgeon once explained to me that she was overwhelmed by the clogged drains, the oven that was not working properly, and all the other things that go wrong around a home. The husband (surgeon) brushed it all aside explaining, "I need to be concerned about the next day's surgery and saving the lives of my patients. I can't be bothered by your piddley little things." This comment can only cause the wife to feel piddley, little, and unimportant. For a homemaker who has been listening to children all day, it is important that she be able to talk to her husband when he comes from work. Unfortunately, we find that the average man speaks twenty-five thousand words a day and the average woman thirty thousand. However, by the time a husband arrives home, he has spoken his twenty-five thousand and his wife has not started on her thirty thousand.

As important as it is for a husband to recognize the type of world in which his wife lives and the particular need she has for support and encouragement, it is also important that wives recognize the type of world in which their husbands live. Husbands frequently work under competitive and difficult circumstances which cause them to become extremely sensitive. Many men say they are subjected to continual criticism at work. There is continual haranguing in many factories, shops, and offices. A man is teased if he wears a new shirt and his cohorts might refer to him as "the fashion show." On the other hand, if he wears the same shirt for two consecutive days, it is suggested that his wife runs the show at home and that she uses all the money to buy clothes for herself.

Husbands and wives must recognize the effect the world of work has upon each other. With this recognition, they can develop an idea of the type of support and encouragement that is required.

St. Paul advises that we clothe ourselves "with heart-felt mercy, with kindness, humility, meekness, and patience." (Colossians 3:12) When my wife and I were married, my father-in-law turned and advised, "Be nice to each other." Since I had been graduated from college the week before our wedding and "knew most of what needed to be known," I paid little attention to the advice of this "old man." It was not until some years later that I remembered and realized the impact of his comment. We often fail to be nice to our spouse. It seems that we take an undue license with him saying things that we would not say to anyone else. We expect our spouse to understand our bad moods and to absorb the anger and disappointment which we vent upon him. It is as though spouses become captive scapegoats. If we get up in an ornery mood, our spouse is to understand that we are not a morning person and that we cannot talk before we have had our coffee. If we are ornery and out of sorts in the evening, our spouse is supposed to understand that we have had a bad day.

Spouses frequently complain that they never knew they had a bad temper until after marriage. They explain they were very calm before marriage, that they are calm with others, and they cannot understand why they are so ornery with their spouse. One of the several explanations for this phenomenon is that one's friends and associates will not tolerate being treated in the abusive way one treats their spouse. Frequently, one only mistreats someone who will take it. Perhaps spouses should refuse to accept abusive treatment from each other. It is often effective for a spouse to be reminded that the other is not going to take the abuse being dished out.

It must be remembered that when man was lonely, God did not provide him with ten cronies, but with one wife. However, we often fail to treat our spouse as well as we treat our friends. A clergyman once advised a couple whose marriage he was witnessing to not treat each other like husband and wife. Instead, he explained, "Treat each other as best friends." The unfortunate implication of this advice was that we take an unfair license with our spouse. In a very simple way, I believe that one of the purposes of marriage is to be nice to each other.

We frequently feel it is foolish to verbally affirm our love for each other or to non-verbally manifest this love. Even though it becomes something one says each day, a couple's love is validated when they repeat that they love each other. In the same way, even though it becomes automatic, it is conducive for a good marriage that spouses continue to hug and kiss each other as they did before they were married. A couple once came to the office of a marriage counselor. The wife tearfully explained that her husband did not love her anymore. The husband was shocked by this remark explaining, "What do you mean? I told you twenty years ago that I loved you and I have never taken it back." One needs to hear this verbal affirmation more often than once every twenty years.

We become equally careless about physical affection. A woman explained to a marriage counselor that she felt neglected and unwanted. The counselor immediately recognized that she needed doses of T. L. C. (tender loving care.) He helped the wife from her chair, held her closely, and gave her a "hydraulic kiss." The counselor turned to the husband explaining, "There, Mr. O'Brien, that is what she needs every Monday, Wednesday, and Friday." The husband replied, "Fine, Doc, I can bring her in every Monday and Friday, but on Wednesday she will have to get in on her own."

One woman explained that her husband received many business calls at home. She could always tell when her husband was talking to a woman. His voice was softer, more flirtatious, and the conversation lasted longer. She explained that she did not so much resent the way he talked to other women, she only resented that he did not talk in this same way to her. This nonsupportive situation caused one wife to explain to me that she could understand why some men went to prostitutes. She thought it would be so good to have someone treat you nice that one might even be willing to pay someone to do so.

Small talk is a very important part of the supportive ingredient. Husbands and "sensitivity buffs" are the worst denigrators of small talk. Husbands exclaim they cannot be bothered with little things and "sensitivity buffs" exclaim that "we have to get down to the gut-level issues." In reality, small talk serves to validate each other's existence, initiates in-depth communication, and helps develop a sense of closeness which aids couples in their efforts to combat feelings of alienation. Small talk is simple conversation about the day, one's feelings, and one's dreams and aspirations.

Because of the lack of a supportive element and the discomfort with small talk, couples feel "lost when they are alone together." Waiters often comment that they can identify married couples because they do not talk with each other. Although couples can experience great solace simply from being together, it may be well to develop the facility to talk with each other. Frequently, husbands tend to be "thing oriented," believing that if one isn't talking about *some thing* such as the car, hunting and fishing, or the world series, it really isn't important. This caused one woman to explain to a marriage counselor that the small talk between her and her husband kept getting smaller and smaller.

In developing the facility for small talk, spouses need to be like the news analyst as compared with the newscaster. The newscaster simply gives the facts as they are, whereas the news analyst tends to get underneath the facts explaining their impact and implications. The newscaster is like the depot agent in the early 1900's who had a habit of sending long detailed reports of train derailments to his superiors. The superiors tired of reading these long reports. They advised the agent to just give them the facts. The next time there was a derailment, the superiors received the following telegram, "Off again, on again, gone again. Finnegan." Rather than to be like the "reformed Finnegan," we need to embroider and enlarge our conversation so that our spouse becomes aware of more than the bare facts. Small talk provides couples with the opportunity not only to be with each other, but to be truly available to each other. There is a difference between being around and being with our spouse. When we are simply around him, we may only be aware of him, but when we are with him, we are available to him. This availability enables us to cope with some of the routine of marriage that is conveyed in the Couple's Prayer:

> In the face of routine
> Let us find new joys.
> When one feels forgotten
> Let us recall love's needs.
> When each of us feels alone
> May we be open enough to share.
> When we feel nothing at all
> Let us rekindle our love.

> (Author Unknown)

Another important dimension of supportive communication is the need for spouses to help each other to feel exclusive. In view of the impersonal nature of our world, it is important that spouses not lose sight of and contact with each other in social situations. They need to develop the ability to cast meaningful glances toward each other, initiate little touches during the course of an evening, and generally to let it be known they are husband and wife and they feel very important to each other.

Norman Vincent Peale[1] explains that people ought to be

---

[1]Norman Vincent Peale, "Pass A Good Word Along," *Reader's Digest,* (June, 1972), pp. 203-209.

relay stations for the little sparks of good will that otherwise might never jump the gap that separates people. He explains he has trained himself to listen for any word of approval or praise that one individual speaks about another—and to pass it on. He mentions that some people find it difficult to pay a compliment directly; to do so embarrasses them. One man explained to a group of friends that his wife was the kindest person he had ever known. A member of the group passed this remark on to the man's wife. Her face grew radiant. "Oh, thank you," she said. "He would never be able to say that to me!" The more often little flashes of good will are released into the environment, the more all the pollutive emotions of fear, hostility, and loneliness are diminished. An Arabian proverb puts it neatly: "Blessed is he who speaks a kindness; thrice blessed is he who repeats it." We do not have to adhere to the philosophy conveyed in the comment, "Beware the flatterer; he feeds you with an empty spoon." As people often comment, "Flattery will get you everywhere."

Frequently when couples entertain for dinner or when they are at a banquet, spouses are asked to sit next to someone else to initiate more stimulating conversation. One should question whether or not having husbands and wives sit next to each other is all that stifling to conversation. I have been the guest speaker at many banquets where this practice was in vogue. Occasionally, I have noticed a husband object to this procedure explaining, "I don't see very much of my wife. This is an excellent chance to be with her and I prefer to sit next to my wife."

Husbands and wives should make an effort to look for what is right within their relationship, to look for what is right about the other, to accentuate the positive, and to compliment each other. Spouses frequently comment that compliments should come spontaneously and one should not have to think about making compliments. This is false reasoning. We are so prejudiced against giving compliments that we must make an effort to do so until complimenting the positive becomes as much a pattern of our life as accentuating the negative.

In fact, we are not only conditioned not to give compliments, but some people have difficulty receiving compliments. It seems that supportive stroking contradicts their Not OKness. Because of their difficulty believing they have any attributes worth complimenting, they are embarrassed by the supportive comment. The validity of this comment must be denied or brushed aside. On the other hand, there are those who become outright suspicious of someone who compliments them. They wonder, "What is he up to?" "What is he trying to get from me?" One of the underlying themes of this book is that spouses act as teachers for each other. They help each other become more deeply aware of the demands of marriage and of the meaning of the interaction of the two personalities within the marriage. In helping each other to become aware of their own need for supportive communication, spouses frequently comment: "What good is it if I have to tell him to be nice to me?" I encourage people not to place themselves or their spouse in this difficult bind in which the unaware or offending spouse is "damned" whether he changes or not. Spouses must accept their role as teacher, help the other become aware of their deep personal needs, and be open to a modified behavior on the part of the previously unaware or offending spouse. A person should not be condemned for not doing what he had not realized he should do. When he "sees the light" and shows a willingness to meet more complicated human needs, his efforts should be encouraged rather than derided because of a "you should have done that without my having to tell you" mentality.

The image people have of themselves is much like a balloon. If people hear good things about themselves, they feel good and their image is inflated. If people do not hear good things, their image may remain the same. If bad things are heard, the image may be deflated. One woman explained that she and her husband were preparing to go out one evening. The husband spontaneously commented that she looked very nice. This made her feel very good and he went on to comment that he appreciated the way she was wearing her hair. The compliments continued and while they were driving to meet their friends, the husband took the hand of his wife, pulled her close to him, and said, "You're a wonderful gal! Thanks for being my wife." By this time, her self-image (balloon) was inflated to full capacity and she felt on top of the world. Later in the evening, the husband explained to the friends that he had a most interesting experience earlier in the day. He went to confession and for his penance, the priest advised him to compliment his wife three times before the day was over. "Pop!" went her balloon.

Although it is important to make supportive comments, it should not be looked at as a penance. However, since we often discover who we are by the way in which we are treated, it must be worked at until it becomes a spontaneous habit. We sometimes become what we are as a result of how we are held by others. To some extent, what we do to another gives them their name and helps to establish their worth in their own eyes. Although spouses may complain that kissing each other and saying they love each other becomes only a routine habit, it may not be such a bad habit!

CHAPTER 9

Talking Without Words

There are many forms of communication (getting the message through), and many ways of expressing feelings, inner thoughts, hopes, desires, and disappointments. The pouting wife and the silent husband, the set of the shoulders, tears, the toss of the head, the frown, the twinkle of the eye, the restless hand, the clenched fist, the rigid body, the swinging foot, the flash of the eyes, and the smile are all nonverbal methods of communication. In the same way, the indifferent, bored, hopeless, or what's-the-use-anyway tone of voice becomes a nonverbal way of conveying a message. Spouses are frequently unaware of the significance attributed to their tone of voice. There are many nuances implied by the way in which one says something. Depending upon the particular situation, spouses use their professional voice, everyday voice, Sunday voice, sexy voice, talking with women voice, or talking with men voice. In many marriages, the spouses only use their everyday voice when speaking to each other. Somehow, it does not occur to many that one's spouse would like to be spoken to with the Sunday voice. There are times when what a person says with his body betrays what he is saying with his tongue. Sigmund Freud once wrote, "No mortal can keep a secret. If his lips are silent, he chatters with his fingertips; betrayal oozes out of him at every pore." Will

Henry of the New York News syndicate explained, "The eyes shout what the lips fear to say."

The importance of nonverbal messages is illustrated by Manfred Clynes[1] who explained that he took part in Pablo Casals' master classes. One day when Casals was teaching a Hayden cello concerto, he asked a participant, a young master in his own right, to play the theme from the third movement. His playing was expert, sure, and graceful, but for Casals, something was missing. Casals stopped the performance exclaiming, "No, no, no! That must be graceful!" With this, the master took up his own cello and played the passage. It was a hundred times more graceful than the audience had just heard. It seemed as though the participants had never heard grace before. Clynes explained they had experienced one of the least understood forms of human communication—a colorful and clear transmittal of feeling without words. Casals played the same notes and at a similar speed, but the nonverbal message was distinctly different.

Messages are communicated when dinner is never ready on time or a husband is never on time for dinner. A messy home and an unfixed faucet are nonverbal messages. Tennyson has said that each person has a language even though it is nothing but the prolonged, sad cry of helplessness. Language, whatever language, reflects accumulated desires, disappointments, hopes, hurts, satisfactions, ambitions, and joys.

A man may successfully control his face and appear calm, self-controlled, unaware that signs of tension and anxiety are leaking out. Rather than be betrayed by our voice, rage may be expressed with our feet or legs. As we explore non-verbal communication, we quickly realize that language is a small part of the way in which we communicate. George du Maurier wrote, "Language is a poor thing. You fill your lungs with

---

[1]Manfred Clynes, "The Sentic Passions at Your Fingertips," *Psychology Today,* (May, 1972), p. 59.

wind, and shake a little slit in your throat and mouth, and that shakes the air; and the air shakes a pair of little drums in my head . . . and my brain seizes your meaning in the rough. What a round-about way and what a waste of time." Flora David[2] comments that communication between human beings would be just that dull if it were all done with words.

Although about seventy percent of our total message is conveyed nonverbally, it is the least understood and least frequently discussed area of marital communication. Couples are affected by nonverbal communication and unconsciously recognize its importance. However, it is an abstract form of communication that spouses most frequently do not translate for each other. Although we are aware of the nonverbal messages emitted by our spouse, we are frequently unaware of our own nonverbal messages. In spite of the awareness of the nonverbal messages transmitted by our spouse, we often do not know how to interpret the message. Since we operate from a negative orientation, we frequently interpret the messages as being negative and assume we have done something wrong. If our spouse grimaces, we assume we have offended her. It does not cross our mind that she might be upset by someone else. Rather than check out the meaning of the message, we may withdraw, wondering what we have done. An equally ineffective alternative is to respond to the assumed anger by becoming angry ourselves.

Since nonverbal messages are abstract and open to a broad range of interpretations, it becomes necessary to check out the meaning of the message. Once in a therapy group, a wife began to say something, her husband looked at her and the wife stopped talking. I asked her to continue, but she explained there was no use talking as her husband became angry about anything she said. When she disagreed with my opinion

---

[2]Flora David, "How To Read Body Language," *Reader's Digest*, (December, 1969), pp. 127-130.

that he had only looked at her to show interest, I discovered the men thought his expression was inquisitive and the women thought he was angry. The husband, himself, explained he was only looking at her to hear what she was going to say. The couple had been married for twenty-two years and many discussions were unresolved as a result of the wife's inaccurate perception of her husband's nonverbal messages.

The above example not only suggests that it is difficult to translate the nonverbal message, but that there are often discrepancies between what one says and how he says it. We can consider the principle of exteriorization which involves the effort to express the emotions exteriorly that are being experienced interiorly. This principle recognizes that there is often an inconsistency between what one feels interiorly and what one's friends, colleagues, and associates see expressed exteriorly. The individual expressing the feelings is generally unaware of the inconsistency between his interior and exterior feelings. Because of the inconsistency, people do not react to him in the way he thinks they ought to react. For instance, one might, interiorly, be feeling very sad. Exteriorly, he may convey himself in a jovial manner. The individual involved believes that the sad feelings are being conveyed and feels rejected when the other person reacts to him as though he is happy. In the same way, the individual may, interiorly, feel angry. Again, the exterior emotion may be one of indifference. The individual is confused when people just seem to be brushing him aside and not taking him seriously. Although it is recognized that all of our emotions cannot show and be expressed, it is generally helpful if there is some consistency between our interior and exterior feelings. At any rate, it becomes necessary that we be aware of the inconsistency between the interior emotions and the feelings which are being expressed exteriorly. For instance, if a husband asks his wife if it is all right with her if he goes on a weekend fishing trip and if she replies, "Yes, it's o.k.," but if there are tears in her eyes and her shoulders are drooping, there is a discrepancy between what she is saying and how she is saying it. This causes a double message which is difficult to translate. Adaptive communication requires that the two levels be congruent so that only one message is communicated.

Another frequently used nonverbal message is the chesire grin. I first identified this phenomenon during the course of an interview in which the wife was becoming increasingly upset. For a few minutes, I lost visual contact with the husband. I asked Judy why she was becoming so upset. She explained that whenever she was upset about something, Bob only laughed at her. I turned and glanced at Bob. Sure enough, his face was filled with a broad "chesire grin." When I asked him why he was grinning, he continued grinning, but explained, "I'm not grinning." As Judy and I explained to him that he was, indeed, grinning, he began to realize why he had had some difficulties earlier in his life. He explained that he could never understand why sergeants in the military always threatened to wipe the grin off his face. He was totally unaware of his grin.

In a time of crisis, we all resort to some type of protective action. Some sound the charge and become aggressive; others sound the retreat and withdraw; others don't know what to do and so they grin. By and large, we are unaware of the nonverbal message being emitted.

The raised eyebrow is another frequently unrecognized nonverbal message. One spouse may back down from a conflict situation explaining that the other spouse is becoming too angry. Until she points out the slight elevation of the eyebrow, observers may be unable to understand why she feels her spouse is becoming angry.

If a couple has an argument during the day and goes to bed still angry, one may toss and turn, unable to get to sleep. The other may turn on his side falling asleep immediately. The insomnic spouse continues to toss and turn becoming increasingly upset and convinced that the sleeping spouse doesn't care one bit. "After all, if he cared one little bit, he wouldn't be able to sleep like a baby." Again, we all handle our feelings in a different way. Some may become upset and manifest the upset by tossing and turning. Others may become upset, but manifest the upset by retreating into sleep. The restless spouse should remember that the sleeping spouse is every bit as upset, but that the upset is being handled in a different manner.

On one occasion, while explaining this concept to a group, an unusually large group of young men nodded in agreement. During the break, I asked them why this particular point had such a strong meaning to them. They explained they had all been in Vietnam where they were faced with overwhelming and frustrating situations; yet they found they were sleeping ten to twelve hours a day. Now, they realized sleep was a form of withdrawal and withdrawal was a way of handling their frustration.

Crying is another frequently misunderstood dimension of nonverbal communication. Frequently, during interviews, a wife will begin to cry. I generally continue talking only to find that the husband begins to answer for his wife. I explain that she can answer for herself. The husband may retort, "You're being mean. Look at her, she's crying. Now leave her alone." I continue talking explaining that she will be able to talk through her tears. After several minutes, the crying subsides and the husband leans back exclaiming, "My God, I never thought you could talk with a woman while she was crying." The wife responds, "Thank goodness you finally realized you don't have to walk out on me when I begin crying."

Wives do not necessarily use crying as a means of manipulating their husbands. It is simply a way of dealing with their emotions. They find it is simpler to cry than develop ulcers.

It is helpful for husbands to learn how to deal with crying. In some instances, a wife may want to be left alone. However, more often than not, she wants her husband to stay with her and to continue talking out whatever is upsetting her or bothering the two of them.

As much as it is necessary for husbands to understand crying, it is necessary for wives to understand grunting. What crying means to a woman, grunting may mean to a man. A husband may come home from work looking like Atlas—having the weight of the world on his shoulders. His wife will ask him what's wrong and he grunts, "Nothing." He then stalks off to bed for an hour. The fact that he is upset is obvious. His refusal to put the nonverbal message into words is unfortunate.

Nonverbal communication is not only used to express hurt, disappointment, and anger, but also in an affirmative and healing manner. There is something healing in touch. Jesus touched people, especially when he was ready to perform a miracle. Touching can become very important to spouses. It is reassuring to feel the touch of the other spouse on one's shoulder. We like to hold, touch, and caress babies and younger children. However, once children enter elementary school, we stop touching them. The underlying thought seems to be that they are now too old for that. I have had many situations in my office where parents and children have broken down the barriers to understanding each other, been overwhelmed by a good feeling toward each other, and then embraced. The teen-age sons and daughters have frequently commented, "That's the first time you've touched me since I was a child." Many teen-agers express their regret that their parents will no longer touch or hold them. Of course, many parents have expressed the regret that their teen-age sons and daughters will no longer let them touch or hold them.

Touch seems to be associated with combat and sexual passes or arousal. We have all grown up hearing, "Don't touch!" The idea that one does not touch is deeply imbedded in many of our minds. Also, it has been demonstrated that children can literally die from lack of touch. The Marasmus syndrome was identified in a Boston Hospital where it was noticed that, for an unexplained reason, several young babies were dying. As they sought to explain the problem, it was noted that these were the babies of unwed mothers who were going to be placed for adoption. These babies were not receiving the tactile care of the other infants. To combat the problem, the hospital hired women whose job was simply to hold and caress the babies.

H. F. Harlow, psychologist at the University of Wisconsin, has done several experiments with monkeys. He has reaffirmed the importance of touch, finding that the baby monkey prefers to lie with a surrogate mother who is covered with soft terry cloth as compared with a wire surrogate mother who has milk. The baby monkeys would take their feeding from the wire mother and go immediately to lie with the terry cloth mother.

Also, as a result of the difficulty many have with touching, it is possible to hold people away from us. One can often be embraced by another and feel that the purpose of the embrace is to hold away and to prevent physical contact.

The importance of touch is demonstrated by a couple who experienced a serious tragedy. Myrna was unconscious for several days during which time Mylan sat by her side holding her hand. When she recovered, Mylan explained that it was reassuring to hold her hand and realize she was still alive. Myrna mentioned that the sense of his presence was reassuring. A friend of ours who had been married for forty-five years was near death. He called his tearful wife to the side of his bed saying, "Sit down beside me, hold my hand, and you won't feel so bad."

Nonverbal communication is used to convey both positive and negative messages; therefore, spouses must clarify the meaning of each other's nonverbal messages. Through this process of clarification, the couple becomes better able to define and cope with what is happening between them. It is also important that couples become aware of the curative effect of nonverbal contact. They need to be aware of the powerful impact of a reassuring glance, a touch on the shoulder, and a squeeze of the hand. Sometimes, it is during the silent moments that couples say the most meaningful things of all.

CHAPTER 10

Being Agreeably Disagreeable—
A Rose By Any Other Name. . . . .

Although couples experience various problems and different intensities of conflict, differences of opinion are a real part of marriage. Spouses cannot expect to agree upon everything. I have previously suggested possible psychological and sociological explanations for marital conflicts. On the other hand, our differences as human beings help us understand that the opinions, aspirations, and desires of spouses will differ. We are created as uniquely different individuals.

Much of the marital advice that is given to couples centers around conflict and problems. Here and there one finds rules for fighting in marriage and the suggestion that fighting is good for a couple—it is like a sneeze, it "clears the passages." The comment that all is fair in love and war, and marriage is a bit of both, has damaging implications. Marriage should not be looked upon as warfare.

Although husbands and wives ought to disagree and resolve differences, they should not fight. The words we use determine the way in which many of our messages are interpreted. Thus, when the reader thinks about a *rose,* a specific thought comes to his mind and he is enveloped by a particular feeling. One may think of a pleasant summer morning, a romantic evening, a wedding, a pleasant aroma, or many other enchanting thoughts. The importance of semantics is demonstrated if the reader now thinks of *weed.* A different thought comes to mind and he is enveloped by quite a different feeling. The same difference applies when couples are advised to fight rather than being advised to constructively resolve their differences.

If couples are advised to fight, a destructive and hostile mental image is aroused. On the other hand, if couples are advised to recognize, deal with, and resolve their differences, a more cooperative mental image is aroused. If couples think of fighting, they often think of hurting the other, winning, and "going in for the kill." I am very uneasy with Virginia Satir's[1] suggestion that, "Fighting is better than being bored. You might get killed, but at least you feel alive while it is going on." If, instead of fighting, the couple thinks of resolving differences, they generally think of discussion, which may very well become heated, but is not primarily designed to hurt and conquer.

Couples should become comfortable with the notion of disagreement and tension. It is part of the romantic love myth that people in love do not quarrel. Spouses need to expect ups and downs in their marriage. A symphony could never be played with only one note. Since differences are a fact of life, it is necessary for couples to learn how to disagree in an agreeable fashion. This is exemplified by the husband who came home in a terrible mood. Noticing that his wife was not in the best of spirits, he exclaimed, "Don't tell me any bad news, I only want to hear the good news." "Well," she said, "you know our five children?—four of them did not break an arm today." In seeking to resolve disagreement and tension, it is not a question of who is going to throw the first stone. Instead, it is a question of who is going to start building with it. Management of disagreements depends, on the one hand, upon the ability to negotiate, bargain, and cooperate, but to a great extent, it depends upon the motivation to continue the marriage.

---

[1]Virginia Satir, *Peoplemaking*, (Palo Alto, California: Science and Behavior Books, Inc., 1972), p. 58.

Couples realize that marriage is not a relationship which contains no hurts. It is not a mutual protection society. Tension in marriage is not bad, but it is necessary to develop a creative approach to resolving disagreements. Couples who do not develop the ability to disagree creatively develop senseless little islands of secrecy in which taboo topics must be avoided. Before long, there is not very much that does not fall into the taboo category.

We are told in Scripture that we should not worry excessively about differences. God not only gave us free wills, but he also created us as distinctly different individuals. Shortly after the death of Jesus, Matthew found it necessary to tell his people how to handle conflict. We should be less concerned about the fact of conflict and more concerned that we effectively integrate the Christian virtues of love and forgiveness.

Couples should first of all accept differences as a part of marriage. However, they should try to disagree agreeably and creatively. So far, this book has emphasized the necessity of viewing marriage as a vocation, it has stressed the importance of understanding one's personal sensitivities as well as those of one's spouse. It has emphasized the supportive and stroking dimension of marriage. Only when these dimensions are placed into a creative perspective can couples trust each other enough to drop their defenses, disagree agreeably, and become able to accept criticism from each other. If spouses are to grow as individuals and as a marital dyad, it will be necessary to give and receive criticism. However, we find that many people would rather die from praise than be saved by criticism. In *The Cart and The Horse,* Louis Kromberger explains that, "Many people don't want honest answers so far as honest means unpleasant or disturbing. They want a soft answer that turneth away anxiety." Winston Churchill said, "Criticism may not be agreeable, but it is necessary. It fulfills the same function as pain in the human body; it calls attention to an unhealthy state of things." The philosopher Solon, who wrote in the fifth and sixth centuries before Christ, advised, "In giving advice, seek to help, not to please, your friend." For criticism to be constructive, it must be like rain—gentle enough to nourish a man's growth without destroying his roots.

Where spouses are concerned, love without criticism brings stagnation—and criticism without love brings destruction. The French have a saying which is translated to mean, "The tune makes the music." The tone of our criticism determines whether its affect will be positive or negative. We need to seek to be like the mother who had four children who did not break an arm. In another family, the children of a very prominent father decided to give him a book of their family's history. The biographer hired for the job was warned of one problem—Uncle Willie, the black sheep, had gone to the electric chair for murder. The biographer reassured the children that this would be handled discreetly. He wrote that, "Uncle Willie occupied a chair of applied electronics at one of our leading government institutions. He was attached to his position by the strongest of ties. His death came as a true shock." The biographer found a way to deal constructively with a touchy issue.

The ability to be constructively critical of each other is based upon a feeling of trust and a belief that the other's primary interest is in helping rather than winning. It is not pessimistic to view conflict as a part of marriage. Perhaps it is true that a pessimist is an optimist with experience; however, I am always concerned when I talk with engaged couples who believe that if they truly love each other, they will never have a disagreement. During the course of a workshop with engaged couples, a fiancee became very upset with my remarks about disagreement. She angrily explained that it was ludicrous to have such a negative view of marriage and for me to suggest that couples should develop ways of dealing creatively with disagreement. She went on to explain that if she and her husband-to-be were going to have disagreements, they would not be getting married. Before leaving the session in tears, she explained they intended to have a good marriage—free of difficulties, disagreements, or conflicts. Many young couples become disillusioned about their disagreements, believing this is an indication they were not intended for each other. Rather than seek to resolve their differences, they conclude their marriage was not meant to be and they seek divorce. The myth of a tension-free marriage is another one of the explanations for trial marriages. Couples wanting to be certain they will have a happy and rewarding marriage test each other in trial marriages. They fail to realize that one cannot give a try at marriage. To be successful, full commitment is required.

In some situations, withdrawal and avoidance become effective ways of dealing with differences. Couples are often admonished: "Do not let the sun set upon your anger." If all couples followed this advice, many would have to stay up all night and fight. There are occasions when pulling back and not dealing directly with a situation is constructive. A couple suggested to me that whenever they became angry and upset with the other, they would say, "Halt." They went on to explain that each letter had a special significance:

> H = Hungry
> A = Angry
> L = Lonely
> T = Tired

This couple realized that if they were hungry, they could not discuss sensitive issues. If they were angry and over-reacting, they realized that one of their sensitive spots had been struck. They then considered these sensitivities before continuing the argument. They realized that if one was lonely, he might be feeling dejected. Perhaps it was best to do something directly about the loneliness rather than to argue about falderal. If they were tired, they also recognized this was no time to discuss sensitive issues.

This couple recognized that there were certain moods and feelings which contra-indicated the discussion of sensitive marital issues. People become unduly suspicious and sensitive when they are tired. This is not necessarily sweeping differences under the rug—a good night's sleep often does wonders for a couple. An issue which may have been impossible to discuss while they were tired, becomes more workable when one is rested. This phenomenon casts doubt upon the advisability of marathon sessions which are sometimes used as a technique for encounter and sensitivity sessions. One of the goals of marathon sessions is for participants to drop their defenses. It is believed that fatigue facilitates this process. This relaxation of defenses is designed to enable participants to relate more authentically and to come more effectively to grips with the quality of their interpersonal relationships and their intrapsychic makeup. I fear the participants become reactively paranoid and all that is said, perceived, and heard is grossly distorted. In reality, defenses are a part of one's psychic makeup and they are not always dysfunctional.

It is advisable for spouses to be aware of each other's moods. Because of circadian cycles, we are in a constant twenty-four hour rhythmic flux of hormones, moods, strengths, and weaknesses. We sleep and wake, our body temperature rises and falls with our hormones, and this causes a rise and fall of efficiency and libido. Our moods affect the efficiency with which we can approach marital conflict.

It is the wise husband who is aware of the menstrual cycle of his wife. He recognizes that there are certain times in some months where discretion is the better part of valor. It is best to let some issues remain unchallenged. He may notice that there is little he can do that is right. Rather than contend directly with the objections to his behavior, the understanding husband seeks to comfort and console his wife. The effects of premenstrual tension caused one husband to quip, "There ought to be pills for husbands to take during this time."

The chauvinist husband may believe that, "It is all in her head." To some extent, that is true. Premenstrual tension is a result of generalized fluid retention, some of which causes a swelling in the cerebral area which causes headaches. The severity of a woman's premenstrual tension varies from month to month, but it should be recognized that this term denotes a physiological change which occurs in all women during their menstrual cycle. She notices hyperirritability, headaches, nervousness, bloating, weight gain and fluid retention. The symptoms are due to the effects of ovarian hormones late in the menstrual cycle.

Many sensitive husbands recognize that the moods and sensitivities of their wives during pregnancy are best left unchallenged. Warmth and reassurance are more appropriate than confrontation. A couple's only daughter was living with them while her husband was overseas. She was pregnant and at first things went smoothly. Before long, her demands on her mother's time began to get to the mother. On numerous occasions, they exchanged harsh words. After one such quarrel, the daughter left the room crying and the mother was upset for having lost her temper. Needing sympathy, she looked at her husband who had sat through the whole battle without saying a word. His wife asked, "How can you sit there and laugh?" The husband replied, "Well, now you know what it's like to live with a pregnant woman."

The loving husband and wife need to accept the reality of interpersonal differences in thinking and behavior. Yet, they will realize that their perspective is subjective and that there are often several acceptable solutions to a particular problem or differences of opinion. They will not see their disagreements as fights, but rather as opportunities to develop a deeper awareness of and appreciation for each other. They will understand that disagreements are creative if they learn something new about the other, if they provide each other with growth opportunities, and if they arrive at mutual decisions that are more satisfactory than if they had acted without working through their disagreement.

CHAPTER 11

How Not To Resolve Differences

As much as it is necessary to be aware of constructive ways of coping with differences, it is also necessary to be aware of ineffectual ways of dealing with differences. This awareness can help couples avoid the pitfalls often experienced while seeking to resolve disagreements. The reader may recall the distinction between a problem and a conflict discussed in Section II. When a couple is dealing with differences, it is necessary that they know whether they are faced with a problem or a conflict situation. If they are faced with a problem, it is possible to face it together and seek to resolve it in a fairly logical and conscious manner. However, if the couple recognizes they are dealing with a conflict situation, it is necessary to identify the source and type of sensitivities that are involved. Unless this can be accomplished, they will be unable to move to a satisfactory resolution of the conflict.

It is because of the failure to differentiate between problems and conflicts and because of the failure to adequately cope with the etiological basis of conflicts that some couples often resort to ineffectual ways of dealing with their differences. This chapter will discuss the ways in which couples should *not* resolve problems and conflicts.

Umbrage File: The person who keeps an umbrage file does not bother to deal directly with differences. He acts as though he is all-understanding and nothing bothers him. However, it is important to realize that he is not brushing things aside, but only filing them away for later use. This is the same idea identified as gunny-sacking by George R. Bach and Peter Wyden.[1] The filing clerk does not use safety valves which are designed to release pressure when it builds to a dangerous point; thus preventing an explosion. Some gunny-sackers fear disagreement. They want so badly to avoid an argument that they start a fight. That is, they hold things inside until they explode. When one supresses or represses those things which he doesn't want to live with, he doesn't really solve the problem because one cannot bury the problem dead—it is buried alive. It remains alive and active inside of a person.

The gunny-sacker believes that married life teaches one invaluable lesson—to think of things far enough ahead not to say them. The only problem is that he says them some months after he feels them. He is not honest with his own feelings as is true of the spouse who follows the advice that, "Only two things are necessary to keep one's wife happy: First, let her think she is having her way, and second, let her have it."

One should be suspicious of the person who says, "I don't get mad very often, but when I do, watch out!" In reality, he becomes angry, but does not bother to do anything about it until his filing cabinet is filled. At that point, he explodes and drags out all the old gripes which have more than likely been forgotten by the offending spouse. During an interview with an accomplished filer, Margaret threw several daggers at Les. When I asked Les if it hurt, he only explained, "That's the way Margaret is. There's no use trying to change her. I

---

[1]George R. Bach and Peter Wyden, *The Intimate Enemy*, (New York: Avon Books, 1968), p. 19.

understand her and it doesn't make any difference." The only difficulty was that old good natured Les filed things away for six to eight months. He would then go out for an evening of drinking, get home early in the morning, awaken his wife, take out each dagger she had thrown during the previous months, dip it in a bit of poison, and throw it back at her.

A disadvantage of living with the filer is that a spouse doesn't really know when he has offended his spouse. One may have to wait years to find out that one has done something offensive. Many spouses repress their hostility and resentment for years. They do not take a firm stand and seem to permit themselves to be mistreated and to be involved in an unrewarding marriage. They may kick up some mild fuss, but they never actually take an adamant stand in which the other spouse realizes that they mean it when they say they will no longer tolerate the drinking, financial irresponsibility, extra-marital affairs, or the general lack of commitment to marriage. Friends and relatives often admire, or are irritated by, the tolerance of the spouse. However, in the end, the tolerant spouse turns out to be not so tolerating. After some years, he may decide that he has "had it" and that the marriage is over and done with. As the previously recalcitrant spouse realizes the previously tolerant spouse means business, he frequently becomes apologetic, repentent, and promises immediate change. In many instances, this is the first time change has really been foisted upon the recalcitrant spouse. Many people fail to modify their behavior until such modification becomes mandatory. Unfortunately, too much water has gone over the dam. As a result, the "tolerant spouse" has lost any love or respect which he previously felt, he is finished with the marriage, and is not interested in starting over. The risk of the gunny-sacker is that his love may be destroyed before he decides to "speak his piece."

In reality, tolerant spouses should be encouraged to develop the ability to insist on legitimate concerns. No one should permit himself to be intimidated or related to in a dehumanizing manner.

In some respects, marriage is like a bank account. Couples can take no more out than they have put in. This causes a certain inequality in many marriages. One spouse seems to put much more into the relationship than does the other. If we were to view marriage as having a maximum satisfaction potential of ten, we might imagine that if one spouse puts in three degrees of effort and the other exerts six degrees of effort, the marriage will have a satisfaction level of nine or at least four and a half. This is not true. Instead, the marriage has only a satisfaction level of three. This implies that the satisfaction level of a marriage can only be as high as the lowest degree of effort that is put into it. This is similar to the idea that a chain is only as strong as its weakest link. The relationship becomes unequal because one is trying harder than the other. The efforts of the spouse who is trying harder are unrewarded because he cannot realize a degree of satisfaction from the marriage equal to the effort being put into it. A non-neurotic marriage cannot remain viable unless the deposit and investment of each spouse is equal.

Matador Syndrome: This syndrome was demonstrated by a husband who put an emphasis on "keeping his cool." He thought of himself as a matador who sought to remain very calm and cool while his wife worked herself up into a rage. He deftly stepped aside of all her charges sticking little needles in her as she passed under his cape. Finally, when she became exhausted from her rage, he delivered the telling blow.

The Matador places a premium upon his ability to be logical, somewhat silent, and rather aloof. He is aware of all

that is going on and waits until the appropriate moment to
come in for the "kill." Obviously this reaction damages the
growth potential of the marriage. The principle goal of disagreement must be to resolve the problem and not to hurt or
make fools of each other. As well as keeping his own cool,
the Matador can help the other keep her cool and deal with
her frustrated feelings in a way which leads to resolution of
the problem or conflict rather than to "glorious victory."

Sarcasm: A dictum within the mental health profession
explains that expressed anger goes away and repressed anger
comes out elsewhere. Sarcasm is one of the ways in which
repressed anger is subtly expressed. This ineffectual method
is often noticed between couples in social situations. Under
the guise of joking, they cut each other down. Unless it is
played too rough and becomes embarrassing for the onlook-
ers, the game of "knock your spouse" has social approval.
Since the larger society does not take marriage seriously and
since spouses have been assigned the role of scapegoat, observers often gain secondary pleasure from watching the
spouses run each other down.

Sarcasm does not always have to be verbal. For instance,
Gladys ran for a particular political office in her village.
Although Fred never expressed his opinion about her political involvement, he resented it, feeling that she already was
spending too much time away from home. After the election,
Gladys announced, in my office, that she lost the election.
When I encouraged Fred to express his feelings about her
loss, he explained he had opposed her involvement since the
beginning, was happy that she had lost, and he had voted for
her opponent. At this point, she tearfully explained that she
had lost the election by one vote. Old "Silent Sam" did his
wife no favors by keeping his personal feelings to himself.

Another form of sarcasm is malicious obedience. This is a
subservient and hostile adherence to the dictates of the
spouse. The passively hostile spouse does exactly as he is

told, precisely following all instructions making certain that the following of instructions fouls up the effectiveness of the "orders" he has been given.

The Silent Treatment: Silence is another indirect way of dealing with problems that has gained social approval. It is generally agreed that if one has been hurt, the other cannot expect him to talk. In reality, it seems that the grieved spouse would rather suffer than to resolve the problem. The one who has caused the hurt may try desperately to apologize. However, he is given the message that the amount of penance is indeterminate. In the meantime, he is to continue doing penance until the grieved spouse decides that he can be forgiven. For instance, Frank came home on Friday evening and within a few minutes he noticed that he was being given the silent treatment. He asked Helen, "What is wrong?" She passive-aggressively[2] responded, "Nothing!" Frank continued to ask what was wrong. He was given various responses throughout the course of the weekend such as, "If you don't know, I'm certainly not going to tell you," "If you don't know, you really have problems," "I'm too hurt to talk about it," or "Now is not the time to talk about it!" On Sunday evening, after the weekend had been ruined, Frank discovered his transgression—he had not noticed Helen's new hairdo. Other than enjoying the suffering, there may also be an effort to avoid intimacy. Intimacy can be avoided by remaining angry about something and suffering silently. Helen would do well to recall the words of Sirach who advises:

---

[2]Passive-aggressivity denotes the indirect expression of anger. Sarcasm, silence, tardiness, and facial expressions are often used as passive-aggressive ways to express anger. It is very difficult for the receiver to deal with the passive-aggressive expression of anger as one is not certain of the intention of the message. Therefore, the receiver may be reluctant to ask the meaning of these subtle expressions of anger. Also, these indirect expressions are easily denied by the sender who may explain, "I just couldn't help being late" or "You must have misunderstood me."

The trap seizes those who rejoice in pitfalls,
   and pain will consume them before they die;
Wrath and anger are hateful things,
   yet, the sinner hugs them tight.

(Sirach 27:29-30)

She should also recall Peter's question to our Lord: " 'Lord, when my brother wrongs me, how often must I forgive him? Seven times?' 'No,' Jesus replied, 'Not seven times; I say, seventy times seven times.' " (Matthew 18:21-23)

There is also the situation in which one spouse ought to apologize. However, the spouse maintains, "I am too proud to crawl," or "I have never apologized to anyone in my life and I am not about to start now." In most instances, one would think that an ounce of apology would be worth a pound of loneliness.

When both spouses have done something to cause tension, they often ask, "Who should apologize first?" I am reminded of the advice we were given in the United States Air Force. In the military, when an officer of a lower rank meets an officer of a higher rank, the lower-ranking officer is to initiate the salute which is then to be returned by the higher ranking officer. Someone in our class asked, "Who salutes first when officers of equal rank meet?" The response was, "The gentle-man salutes first." Perhaps it is the gentle-man or the gentle-woman who apologizes first in marriage.

Looking To Others For Support: When we are upset and angry about something, we are frequently uncertain of our right to have these feelings. Therefore, we often look to others to find validation for our opinion. For instance, a husband may announce to his wife, "It isn't only me who thinks you are a sloppy housekeeper. While I was driving Mother to the airport last week, even she agreed that you are a messy housekeeper!" Realizing that it is difficult to accept criticism, it must also be recognized that the task of accepting criticism is not made easier by finding out that several others agree that we are inadequate. Conflict resolution is not helped by a wife's comment, "It isn't only me who thinks you're impossible. Even Marian (the next door neighbor) agreed that you have a terrible temper!"

In seeking to resolve conflicts, couples need to own up to and deal with their *own* feelings. Since marital trust is not built when a spouse finds that he is being talked about in the neighborhood or at the office, it is inadvisable to bring other people's opinions into the argument.

Automatic No: In some marriages, the spouses become so careless about their problem solving approach that they do not hear what the other is asking or saying. They seem programed to come forth with an automatic no to any query or comment. They do not know to what it is they are saying no and problems go unresolved.

Predicting the Response: This is another damaging and dysfunctional way of dealing with problems and/or conflicts in marriage. Frequently, the effort of a marriage counselor is to encourage couples to really listen to what the other is saying and doing. Spouses frequently assume that they know each other so well that they can be certain that he is going to be angry, depressed, that he won't be home on time, that he will forget the anniversary, or that he won't want to go out. When spouses *really* listen to each other, they are frequently surprised to find they are in agreement or that the other spouse does not feel, think, or react in the predicted manner. Spouses should do each other the courtesy of listening so as to really hear the other's feelings and opinions.

For some time, I encouraged Phyllis to listen to what her husband said rather than to predict his responses. During one interview, she explained to her husband, "You surprised me." The husband asked, "Why?" To this Phyllis replied, "Probably it is because you did not say what I thought you were going to say." She was beginning to listen.

One of the techniques used in teaching Morse Code has been to deliberately give the trainees incomplete sentences. The instructors found that the trainees completed the sentences in their own way and they swore to the high heavens that that was the message dictated to them. We predict responses according to our own prejudices and predilections.

Couples who have been married for twenty to twenty-five years are particularly prone to predicting the response. They assume, "We have been married so long that I don't even have to ask him what he wants or what he is thinking. I know his every want and thought." If these predictions are right, the couple may get along quite well. However, there is a better than fifty percent chance that the predictions are wrong. If the predictions are wrong, the predicted spouse may never bother to correct the error. Instead, he will assume, "She never seems to do what I want her to do. I guess she really doesn't care very much about our marriage." The dangers of this type of carelessness caused one man to quip, "Intuition is what enables a wife to contradict her husband before he says anything." In some marriages, the spouses never really seem to complete a sentence. As they begin to say something, the other says, "You don't have to say it, I know what you're going to say."

During one of my visits with my parents, my mother answered the phone, talked briefly, saying, "Ah, huh. Ah, huh. Thanks for calling." She then turned to my dad and said, "Whatchamacallit called and whatzisname is in the hospital." My dad simply grunted an, "Oh." If he knew who whatchamacallit and whatzisname were, their communication was effective. However, if he predicted inaccurately, some friend was hurt that he did not receive a get well card and another friend wondered how the story got started that he was sick in the hospital.

Careless prediction of responses is also a risk of the newly married when they assume their love enables them to know the slightest wish and desire of their spouse. Since love knows all, the spouses do not bother to check with each other, they make erroneous predictions, feelings are hurt, and the process of alienation is established.

Since husbands frequently comment that, "Women are unpredictable," they ought to be more certain to validate the predictions they have about their wives. On the other hand, wives ought to have very little faith in their intuitive powers.

Throwing Up Hands: Another ineffectual way in which couples sometimes deal with their disagreements is to fallaciously assume the problem cannot be resolved, throw up their hands, and walk away exclaiming, "I never could talk with you!" or "you're just like your mother and no one can talk with her either!" or "It's impossible to talk with you without your getting mad!"

The throwing up of hands is ineffectual because it is often resorted to before there is any serious effort exerted toward resolving the difficulty. The one who throws up his hands generally does not want to resolve the tension. The existence of the tension prevents intimacy and provides a fallacious validation that the other person is impossible or that the relationship contains insoluble problems.

The Right To Feelings

Many of the spouses who use these dysfunctional methods of dealing with disagreement fail to distinguish between having a feeling and acting on it. Although there are some occasions where it might be wrong or dangerous to act on a feeling, it is never wrong just to have a feeling. For example, it might be wrong for a person to hit a spouse, but it is never wrong for him to feel like hitting a spouse. This general principle—that it is never wrong just to have a feeling—may sound very simple, but many people think they should not have certain feelings. For example, some think they should never feel angry—that instead, they should always feel cheerful and loving. In fact, people often go to great lengths to deny that they feel angry, even in situations in which anger seems very reasonable. To demonstrate this, you can try an experiment on your own. The next time someone you know seems obviously angry about something, simply ask him, "Are you angry?" Probably he will immediately deny it—saying something like, "No, I am not angry, I am just a little frustrated," or, "I am just concerned about my rights," or something similar. As human beings, we have a right to all of our feelings. We have a right to feel angry or discouraged or afraid or unhappy, as well as to feel happy or brave or loving. By allowing ourselves to have these feelings without condemning ourselves, we are really allowing ourselves to be persons—for our feelings are part of what makes us a unique, living person.

Expressing a feeling verbally is perhaps midway between simply having a feeling and acting on it. By expressing a feeling verbally, one is, in a sense, providing an outlet for it without physically acting upon it. For this reason, expressing a feeling verbally is often the most constructive thing one can do with it. For example, suppose a person is feeling angry at someone. It might be wrong for him to act on the feeling in a physical sense—but this does not mean he must suppress it. Since acting on physical anger might be wrong and suppressing it might only lead to its expression in a more subtle or destructive form, probably the most constructive thing a person could do is to express the anger verbally. There are two constructive accomplishments when anger is expressed verbally and directly. An outlet is given for the expression of feelings, and the other person is aware of what is bothering the spouse.

When people do not allow themselves to have negative feelings or think that it is wrong to have them, this invariably influences how they express their feelings, if they express them at all. Consider two examples. First, consider a person who thinks he should never feel anger. Suppose he finds himself in a situation in which he does feel angry. Since he thinks it is wrong for him to have this feeling, he may at first try to suppress it. However, if the anger builds up in him enough, he may finally reach the point where he feels he must express it. Because he thinks that he should not have this feeling of anger, he may feel a need to justify it if he expresses it. To do this, he will need to make a case against the other person—to prove that the other person is clearly in the wrong, and thus that his anger is clearly justified. When he does express his feelings, then, how will they be expressed—directly or accusatively? In most instances, the feelings would be expressed accusatively. On the other hand, if a person thinks he has a right to his personal feelings, no matter what they may be, he will not feel a need to justify them. When he expresses his feelings to the other person, he will not be trying to prove that the other person is wrong, but rather, will simply be communicating his anger to the other person. In this way, he will be getting things off his chest, and at the same time, letting the other person know what it is that is bothering him. We would expect that this person would express his feelings directly. If a person feels the need to justify his negative feelings, he will tend to express them accusatively. If he does not feel the need to justify his negative feelings, he will tend to express them directly.

Spouses must also be aware of the complexity of feelings and the effect this complexity has upon communication in marriage. Although we like to think of ourselves as having very clear, straight-forward feelings about things, it is often not the case. It is quite possible to experience more than one feeling at a time—even if the two feelings seem opposed to each other. Consider, for example, the feelings of parents when a child who has run away or gotten lost comes home. The two opposing feelings might have been happiness and anger, or relief and irritation. It is possible for a person to experience more than one feeling at a time, even if these feelings seem opposed or contradictory. At the same time, of course, feelings vary according to degree. One can feel very happy or moderately happy or only slightly happy. Thus, it is easy to see why feelings can be so complex. One can experience more than one feeling at a time and different degrees of these feelings. Rather than being simple, our feelings are often confusing and complex.

The failure to acknowledge the full complexity of feelings can sometimes have an adverse effect upon communication. We can consider some pairs of feelings that people might easily experience simultaneously. You might ask yourself if you have ever experienced any of these feelings, under what conditions the feelings were experienced, and whether you were able to communicate both feelings openly and directly?

Joy and sadness.
Sexual attraction to someone and irritation with him or her.
Interest in something and fear of it.

In order to be able to communicate complex and contradictory feelings openly and directly, it is essential to let ourselves have these feelings. This is often difficult, because, in a sense, it means that we have to let ourselves be irrational. If you like to think of yourself as a "rational" person, it may be difficult to allow yourself feelings which seem contradictory, opposed, and irrational. It should be reiterated that we have a right to all of our feelings, no matter how illogical or irrational they may seem. Allowing ourselves to have these feelings makes it possible for us to express them in their full complexity, and this, in turn, leads to improved communication. Having feelings which seem contradictory is one example of being "irrational." Another is simply having feelings for which there is no readily apparent reason. Occasionally, this happens to all of us—we may suddenly feel happy or depressed or angry or affectionate without any apparent cause. The fact that these feelings seem irrational does not make them any less real. If a person always tries to have a "good reason" for his feelings, communication within the marriage can be disrupted. Suppose, for example, that such a person felt irritated when there was no apparent reason for it. What do you think would happen if he communicated this feeling? How would it be expressed? In the attempt to find a reason for his feeling, the person would probably accuse the other person of having done something to cause his irritation—thus, he would probably express his feelings accusatively.

Stages Of Problem-Conflict Resolution

In seeking to resolve a problem or conflict, couples may go through several stages. In fact, some of these stages may include some of the ineffectual methods discussed above. Rather than to be discouraged by this, couples should seek to move on to more constructive stages. Spouses may initially experience hurt or anger, in the next stage they may not want to talk about the problem or conflict, and in the next stage the wife may cry and the husband may grunt. These stages may be preparatory to arriving at a point of resolution. Spouses may be aware that time mellows people as much as it does wine. Along with recognizing the curative effects of time, we need also to recognize that it takes time to find the appropriate solution to problems and conflicts.

As couples are going through the various stages involved in

resolving difficulties and tensions, they may need to do various foolish things in order to ease the tension. For instance, a husband may get up in the morning, trip over the bowling ball, cut himself shaving, break the shaving lotion bottle, etc. At this point, he recognizes that he has not gotten off to the best start. Rather than to permit the accumulated tension to cause his emotions to escalate out of control, he might be better off to go back to bed and start the day over. Another husband was late getting home and telephoned his worried and angry wife exclaiming, "Don't pay the ransom, I just escaped." Rather than to let the tension snowball, a spouse is better advised to take himself less seriously, to shrug off the difficulty, and to realize that "a brighter day may be ahead." For instance, a husband may be unable to find the car keys as he is ready to leave for work. He may become angry with his wife accusing her of not putting the keys back in the cupboard and he may issue a directive that she will not be permitted to drive the car until she learns to put the keys back where they belong. He gets his coat on to run and catch a ride with the neighbor. As he slams his hands into his coat pocket, out come the keys. If he takes himself too seriously, he becomes very upset about this exclaiming to his wife, "You pulled a trick on me, you hid the keys in my pocket." If he has the ability to laugh at himself, he can say, "Oh well, maybe even God makes mistakes."

There is a knack to disagreeing that all couples should learn. Certain techniques are harmful, others are risky, and others are constructive. If the quarrel has been constructive, the couple should emerge from it with the marriage being stronger than it was in the beginning.

1. Spouses must accept the fact of the conflict without shame or pretending that it is not there. They should remember that conflict is normal. They must face the fact that each is a human being, and not be alarmed when differences arise from time to time.

2. Husbands and wives must try to find out what the whole area of disagreement means to their spouse. What is "eating" him or her? How does he feel about it and why? Spouses must keep as calm as possible while still talking about it.

3. Spouses should know what it matters to them, why are they annoyed or irritated? They must honestly ask themselves why they are so excited.

4. Couples must adopt a problem-solving approach to the situation but keep remembering that many situations need not really become conflicts. On the basis of a mutual acceptance and understanding, spouses should try to see what can be done to work things out comfortably. Couples should not let the tensions build up day after day but instead work out the tensions as they come along.

5. Husbands and wives should try to agree on some next step for taking care of the situation and get busy on it together as soon as possible.

6. Spouses should do what they can to help the other save face, feel stronger, and feel that he is loved, no matter what. It is best to avoid sniping at each other and to focus energy on the problem as much as possible rather than on the other's faults.

7. Couples should try to be patient and willing to take a little time for the solving of difficulties. They should not expect miracles and should plan on spending some time to solve the problems.

In seeking to cope with the traumas experienced in marriage, it is helpful for couples to listen quietly and attentively. In his book, *Listening With The Third Ear,* Theodor Reik discusses the idea of listening for the feelings that are involved in what the other is saying. A woman with whom I was talking had been informed that she had a tragic and fatal disease. As she told me about this, I turned to her husband, who happened to be a physician, and he responded, "Yes, Florence has a most interesting disease." The physician-husband was not tuning into the feelings that were involved. At that point in time, his wife required support and understanding. She had no need to listen to a lecture concerning the interesting features of her disease.

Couples need to become adept at asking themselves, "What goes on here?" In seeking to resolve problems and conflicts, it is necessary to look underneath what is happening in order to better understand what is going on inside of each other. Sometimes competitive feelings hamper the couple's ability to deal competently with their problems and conflicts. The damaging effect of competition will be discussed in the following chapter.

CHAPTER 12

The Neurosis Of Competition

Some of the advice couples read and hear about communication and problem solving falls upon barren ground. One of the reasons is that many spouses are involved in a horrendous competitive relationship. They make of marriage a zero-sum competitive game which ultimately blocks the development of an intimate relationship. It is difficult to develop warm and intimate feelings with your enemy. If one sleeps with his combatant, one eye must be kept open. Competitiveness not only interferes with intimacy, but it also prevents couples from constructively resolving their conflicts and disagreements. Since competing couples are continually keeping score, one spouse fears going along with the other's idea as such agreement would give his spouse another point or two in the total battle. In the same vein, a spouse fears apologizing because that chalks up a score for the other. In another instance, a spouse may refuse to accept an apology because the act of apologizing may give the other a score. Many people operate from a one-up superior position to shore up their own Not OK feelings and to gain some modicum of self-acceptance. Fundamentally, persons who cannot tolerate equalitarian relationships feel unequal. They fear that if they relate on an equalitarian level, they will be smothered by Not OK feelings. To gain relief from their feelings of inferiority, they cash in on the real or projected inadequacies of the

143

other. Rutledge explains that, "One lives most effectively for the joy of living, not for the thrill of conquering. One of the most destructive elements in the culture is neurotic competition."[1] There are both cultural and neurotic explanations for competitiveness in marriage which need to be examined.

The competitive dimension of marriage has been intensified by the various liberation movements. Emphasis is placed upon being one's self and doing one's thing. This often interferes with the development of a cooperative spirit. At the present time, women are admonished not to permit themselves to become the victims of chauvinist males. On the other hand, men are conditioned to fear being dominated by women. They are to be the superior and aggressive sex. Each of these erroneous ideas interferes with personal and marital fulfillment. Since it is no challenge to be either dependent or independent, one of the tasks of marriage is to develop a sense of interdependence. It is easy to let one person make all of the decisions or to be the person who makes all the decisions; however, only mature and healthy spouses can relate on a cooperative and corroborative level. Many couples are involved in a power struggle in which they are not as interested in resolving a problem as they are in proving who wields the power. Essentially, they suffer from the Tareyton Syndrome—they would rather fight than switch.

Our culture conditions us to winning. We have been trained as competitors and a strong competitive element enters into the intimate interpersonal relationship of marriage. Of course, there are several ways in which competition can be helpful and constructive, but in many situations, competition becomes the goal rather than the means to an end. It becomes a goal when one does not focus upon developing effective communication, but instead directs his

---

[1]Aaron Rutledge, *Pre-Marital Counseling*, (Cambridge, Massachusetts: Schenkman Publishing Company, Inc., 1966), p. 2.

efforts to showing his superiority and ability to beat someone else. At this point, there is a risk that the individual's sense of well-being is totally tied up in his ability to beat others. In this way, life together is a competitive game in which the spouses validate their sense of worth by defeating the other. The neurotically competitive person must walk faster than others, get ahead of the line, win all arguments, etc. His dignity and worth are wrapped up in his ability to defeat others.

The competitive spouse is committed to changing people's minds—other people's. He fails to recognize that people are unable to get along unless they are willing to view situations from the viewpoint of another and unless they are sensitive to the feelings and concerns of the other.

It is important for a married couple to reflect upon the many ways in which they have been conditioned to win. This conditioning process begins very early in life; as a girl realizes her parents are pleased when she does better in school than the neighbor girl; as the little league pitcher realizes he is a "better boy" when his team wins; or as the teenager realizes that the boy with the fastest car has more status among his peers.

We are also conditioned to be competitors as a result of the conflict orientation present in our society. As we watch the news, we notice that a futile effort is being made to resolve problems through war, shouting matches, and by the denigration of an adversary's personality.

Vince Lombardi, former football coaching great with the Green Bay Packers is supposed to have said, "Winning isn't everything, it is the only thing." This attitude not only pervades the thinking of athletes, but of our general society. We believe there are two types of people in the world: (1) the winners who always win, and (2) the losers who always lose. Unfortunately, many spouses in marriage seek to prove that one is a winner and the other is a loser. A former baseball star told the story about his wife who had been a high ranking tennis player. He assured her that he would learn to play tennis well enough to beat her. At long last, the day came when the star beat his wife 7-5, 7-5. "And two days later," he added, "our first baby was born." If he could not tolerate being second-best in tennis, one can imagine how difficult it was for him to tolerate any ideas she might suggest. This couple eventually divorced.

Related to the cultural conditioning process is the emphasis placed upon being right. Our society places sacredotal emphasis upon being right. As a result, spouses seem continually to be seeking to prove who is right and who is wrong. For instance, spouses frequently say to me, "Just who do you think is right," or "Now, do you think I'm right or wrong?" Whenever a husband explains to me that he won an argument from his wife, I generally think that was the most recent time the relationship lost a little bit. Husbands often come to my office explaining, "No man should have to live with a woman like this! Don't you agree with me?" His wife may ask, "Don't you agree that a woman should not have to live with a man like him?" When a couple seems only interested in proving who is right and who is wrong, I am inclined to think that the relationship is wrong. In some situations, they may be best advised to seek a divorce, and to have their friends and relatives autograph the divorce decree in honor of their rightness.

Although in an effort to prove their position couples attempt to use logic and reason, very few couples actually argue. Argument is a term used by lawyers and philosophers which implies the use of reason and deals with problems to which there are reasonable solutions. However, most marital disagreements are not very reasonable and do not have objectively right answers. One lawyer was confounded to find that it was futile to argue with his wife. He explained that, "Just when I was able, through my relentless logic, to convince her of the absurdity of her argument—she hauled off and socked me." Couples need to recognize that there is no single correct solution to most marital problems or conflicts. Perhaps Martin Luther recognized the subjectivity of human perception when he explained, "Whoever wants to be a Christian should tear out the eyes of reason because reason is a whore." What appears perfectly logical to one individual does not appear at all logical to the other. For instance, one husband complained to his wife about the dinner she prepared. "What's the matter?" she demanded. "Monday you liked stew, Tuesday you liked stew, Wednesday you liked stew. Now, Thursday, all of a sudden you don't like stew!"

It is difficult to live with someone who continually causes you to feel you are wrong. After a while, a spouse begins to feel he is *really* wrong. That is, that he is a *wrong person*. It would be helpful if spouses followed the advice of this limerick:

> To keep your marriage brimming
> With love in the loving cup
> Whenever you're wrong, admit it
> Whenever you're right, shut up.

Frequently we argue about the rightness of our position explaining that it is a matter of principle. More often than not, it is a matter of pride. Each of us has his own conviction of rightness, and almost by definition the utopian condition of which we all dream is that in which all people finally see the error of their ways and agree with us. It would be healthier for spouses to realize that it may be true that one never makes a mistake, but that errors have a way of creeping in.

It is important to realize that each is right from his own perspective. Nina and George O'Neill explain that three baseball umpires were telling a reporter how they distinguished a ball from a strike. The first umpire said, "There are balls and there are strikes and I call them as I see them." The second umpire explained, "There are balls and there are strikes, but I call them as they are." But, the third umpire replied, "There are balls and there are strikes, but they ain't nothing until I call them."[2]

The perplexing problems confronting the married fall into a gray area. They have *few* right answers, but *many* ways in which they can be coped with. To contend with the disagreements of marriage, one must have the skill of Henry Clay, who has been known as the "Great Compromiser." If one is to find right answers to the problems confronting the married couple, he must have the wisdom of Solomon. If one is ever to judge in marriage, he must have the skill of Portia in Shakespeare's "Merchant of Venice," who declared that Antonio's debt to Shylock did not have to be paid, because Shylock could only have the pound of flesh, and not one ounce of blood, and could in no way endanger the life of Antonio.

Once while explaining to a couple the futility of trying to prove who was right and who was wrong and the necessity of finding adjustments to each other's point of view, they nodded in agreement. However, Mona went on to say that she became very angry when her husband took four-day fishing trips. Tom mentioned that he became very angry when Mona exaggerated so much. He declared that it was a two-day fishing trip and not a four-day trip. I was chagrined thinking that this must certainly be a situation in which one was right and the other was wrong. I asked them to tell me how one could possibly perceive of it as a two-day trip and the other as a four-day trip. Mona said that Tom took off work on Friday and did not return to work until Tuesday.

---

[2]Nina and George O'Neill, *Open Marriage: A New Life Style For Couples,* (New York: Evans Company, Inc., 1972), p. 115.

Tom countered, arguing that he took off work on Friday to get ready for the fishing trip, did not leave until Friday evening, got home late Sunday and spent Monday getting things cleaned up from the trip. Who was right? Was it a two-day trip or a four-day trip?

The fishing trip suggests to us that an argument is frequently the longest distance between two points of view. It often demonstrates that too often we seek justice for just us. It is the subjective nature of marital discord that makes it difficult for spouses to follow Matthew's dictums about fraternal correction. He explains, "If your brother should commit some wrong against you, go and point out his fault, but keep it between the two of you. . . ." (Matthew 18:15) When a spouse judges that he or she has been wronged, he must be certain he is truly listening to the Spirit and not only to his selfish interests. Matthew goes on to say that, if necessary, others should be brought into the matter in order to emphasize the seriousness of the confrontation. If a spouse is going to follow Matthew's advice to the letter and bring others into it (which I suggested in the previous chapter was very dangerous), one again must be very certain he is right or great harm is done. The difficulty is that most people do not really pray over their concerns asking for the power to discern between justice and injustice. Also, we may not fully comprehend the responsibility we have for each other's salvation.

Team work is difficult when spouses enter into the competitive, who-is-right paradigm, or when they seek only to prove that one is better than the other. Spouses are frequently like a group of boys playing basketball who have learned nothing about teamwork. Because of their inability to cooperate, they compete with their own teammates. Four guys get on the one kid who is taking all the shots. He then throws the ball to another kid and says, "O.K., if you're so darn good, you do the shooting." That kid takes some shots, misses, gets the razzberries, and he throws the ball to another

kid saying, "O.K., if you're so darn good, you run the team."
They continue throwing the ball back and forth never learning to cooperate and getting further behind. In marriage, the
situation is similar. A husband may offer some suggestions to
his wife about caring for the children. However, she takes
exception to this saying, "O.K., if you know so much, you
take care of the kids." She stands on the sidelines, watches
his miserable efforts, rides him about his failures, and he
finally gives up saying, "O.K., if you know so darn much,
you do it." The "Here, You Take It" game is often played
with the family budget. It is fairly impossible for any family
to balance their budget. Rather than to cooperate in solving
this difficult problem, many couples choose to compete.
They throw the responsibility for the budget back and forth.
The husband may have responsibility for awhile, the wife
observes his failures, gives him the razzberries, and he finally
says, "O.K., you do it!" He stands on the sidelines, rides her,
spends a little more than he has to just to make sure she
won't be able to do the job adequately, and finally she
throws the budget back to him.

It seems that our sense of self-esteem is wrapped up in
showing that we are better than the other rather than that we
can cooperate with the other. We have learned more about
competing, grandstanding, and taking the sole responsibility
for the show than we have learned about working together.
Spouses need to realize that they are never going to "win the
game" if they keep throwing the ball back and forth.

Competent and accomplished people frequently run the
risk of developing a competitive relationship in marriage.
Each spouse has individual competencies. Both have been
accustomed to doing things autonomously, each of them
has been a "standout," and neither has learned to cooperate.
They may have learned to be the center of attraction (the
Homecoming Queen and Football Captain Syndrome), but
they have not learned to cooperate.

Competitive couples often play the "You Said and You Did" game. These couples seek to prove their rightness by explaining that they did or said something because the other spouse did or said something. Somehow, the other spouse is always proven wrong because of something he said or did. This "You Said" spouse may be like the Gunnysacker who reaches back several years in order to prove his point of view.

Although this chapter has examined socio-cultural and various other conscious factors which condition spouses to compete with each other, the title, "The Neurosis of Competition" implies that the etiological phenomena producing the competitive spirit are unconscious. Essentially, the competitiveness is caused by the unconscious feeling of Not OK-ness, the fear of annihilation, and the carry-over into adult life of the childhood game of "Mine Is Better Than Yours." The competitiveness which infects the culture and affects spouses is caused by the unconscious feeling of inferiority and the desire to preserve integrity.

The tendency to blame others or to prove we are right seems to be a part of human nature since the fall in the Garden of Eden. Adam blamed Eve saying, "She made me do it," and Eve blamed the devil saying, "The devil made me do it." In overcoming the tendency to blame others and the need to prove ourselves right, we overcome a part of the effect of original sin. Spouses need to examine the quality of their interaction and determine the extent to which the relationship contains a destructive competitive dimension. When the competitive areas are identified, the couple should seek to understand the reason they choose to compete. They should then seek to find another basis upon which to relate to each other. The next chapter will discuss various systems of decision making, demonstrating that satisfying decisions can be made only in a cooperative rather than in a competitive atmosphere.

CHAPTER 13

Systems Of Decision Making

Couples can more effectively sort out competitive elements in their relationship if they are able to identify the system or the combination of systems they use in reaching decisions. Couples should develop "meta communication"; that is, they should be able to talk about how they talk. The potential effectiveness of communication is enhanced if couples can define and categorize the way they talk with each other.

This not only helps the couples to enrich their relationship, but when the relationship is not going smoothly, they can analyze the content and style of their communication. In this way, they can identify whether or not they have fallen into the trap of utilizing a system of communication that is dysfunctional for them.

However, since a *philosophy* of communication is most important, couples should not merely focus upon a *technology* of communication. I have attended communication workshops in which the technology of communication becomes a system which enables people to manipulate each other to their own point of view. Although the technique of checking the meaning of another's message by saying, "What I hear you saying is. . .," is useful, it can be used as a way of saying what we wish the person would have said rather than what we actually heard him say. A philosophy of communi-

152

cation which is based upon a recognition of the vocational nature of marriage, acceptance of the egalitarian concept, and a recognition that effective communication leads to knowledge, understanding, and love of the other is the most constructive. Although the authoritarian, bastardized democratic, and syncretic-cooperative processes of decision making will be examined, it will be suggested that the syncretic-cooperative is the most conducive to the development of a rewarding love relationship.

Authoritarian System

The authoritarian system is based upon the premise that males are the superior sex and that females are the inferior sex. One subjugated woman complained that her husband received, evaluated, and vetoed whatever she said. This ineffectual method was demonstrated by Jackie Gleason in his role as Ralph on the *Honeymooners* series which offered many interesting insights into marriage. During one of the programs, Ralph ranted and raved about his superior position. He exclaimed, "A man's home is his castle, I am the lord and the master, you are nothing, you will do what I tell you! I am the king! I am everything! You are nothing." Alice listened silently until he finished. Then, with her arms folded, she looked him in the eye exclaiming, "BIG DEAL! That makes you king of nothing!" This exemplifies what happens if couples utilize the authoritarian system. The subjugated one begins to feel like an old rug that is being walked over. After some years of such treatment, a spouse becomes to feel like nothing. Cher of the Sonny and Cher show wielded the ultimate "put down" to Sonny when he ranted about his superior position claiming he had the better voice, unusually good material, superb relationships with agents, and back-up performers. She looked away and said dryly, "Your fly is open."

If both husband and wife are authoritarian, they become enmeshed in a horrendous power struggle. The fight is the thing. One can never give into the other, apologize, or admit that the other person's opinion is valid. Such admission would give the other spouse points in the all-around conflict. These couples are typically the people who do not let the sun set upon their anger—they stay up all night and fight. They effectively avoid intimacy which may be the fundamental reason for utilizing this ineffectual system.

Other than an unconscious need to avoid intimacy, couples may opt for this system because of the cultural bias which dictates that "a man is to be the boss." The misunderstanding and misapplication of this concept was suggested in the previous chapter and will be discussed in greater depth in the following chapter.

Engaged couples who opt for the authoritarian style may want to use the marriage vows suggested in one of Jules Feiffer's comic strips:

Minister to groom:	Do you take this woman to oppress, subjugate, brutalize, and reduce to a condition of servitude and second-class citizenship?
Groom:	I do.
Minister to bride:	Do you take this man to alienate, dominate, emasculate, and reduce to a state of abject guilt and child-like dependence?
Bride:	I do.
Minister:	I now pronounce you husband and wife. Now! Work it out!

The authoritarian person must recognize that one does not lead by hitting people over the head—that's assault, not leadership. President John F. Kennedy faced this situation when he explained to Nikita Khrushchev: "We cannot bargain from the position that what is mine is mine and what is yours is negotiable." A subjugated husband explained that when he and his wife were initially married, they decided that some of the minor decisions would be made individually; however, all the major decisions were to be discussed mutually. He went on to explain that, "It seems as though, so far, there have been no major decisions in our marriage."

Bastardized Democratic

Modern couples who are imbued with the philosophy that each person must make up his own mind and that everyone must be accepted for what he believes, run the risk of adapting the bastardized democratic process in which they "I don't care" each other to death. When a husband asks his wife if she wants to go to a movie, she replies, "I don't care, it's up to you." When hunting season comes around and he asks her if she minds if he takes another weekend to go hunting with his friends, she replies, "I don't care, it's up to you." Sometime later, he may explain to his wife, "You know, dear, we have been married for twenty years and you really are not 'turning me on' in the way I like. Since I have not felt fulfilled in this marriage, I have found somebody else who really turns me on. Do you mind if we divorce so I can find real happiness?" To this the "democratic" wife replies, "Gee, I don't care dear. Whatever you'd like to do."

Couples frequently drift carelessly into the bastardized democratic process. Rather than to work at making decisions, it is simpler to say, "I don't care, do whatever you would like." After several years, they really *do not* care. Many people simply do not want to go through the hassle of creative decision making. It is much easier to say one doesn't care and to then go ahead and do exactly what you want. Severe feelings of alienation emanate from this system.

Admittedly, there are some situations in which one spouse does not have a definite opinion and in which he prefers that the other would just do what he thinks best. However, in most situations, spouses do have opinions which need to be discussed. There are other situations in which we *ought* to have opinions. There is a most prominent place in hell reserved for spouses who make a virtue out of the "Well, whatever you would like to do" response. They let the other spouse think they are having their way only to proceed merrily in their own direction.

Aaron Rutledge suggests an exchange of vows for couples opting for the bastardized democratic system:

> We, two democratic individuals, desiring to make our abode together, in order to form a more perfect union, establish justice, insure domestic tranquility, provide for the common defense, promote the general welfare, and secure the blessings of liberty to ourselves and our posterity, do hereby unite ourselves in the bonds of matrimony.[1]

Syncretic-Cooperative Process

The ideal system for decision making in marriage is one which is based upon an acceptance of equality, a recognition of the fact that spouses are different, and a commitment to arriving at decisions which are mutually acceptable. In their business meetings, Quakers utilize the syncretic-cooperative system in which votes are not taken and decisions are not made until all are of one mind. For spouses who want quick and instant decisions, the arduousness of this process is undeniable. However, it is a system which helps couples develop understanding, awareness, and love. Couples using this system recognize they will probably begin a discussion with different points of view. They have the deepest respect

---

[1] Aaron Rutledge, *Premarital Counseling,* p. 40.

for each other and believe they each bring uniquely special information and opinions into the decision making process. They realize that if they open themselves up to each other by sharing their information, expressing their beliefs and opinions, and divulging their inner fears and sensitivities, they will arrive at a decision that is more meaningful than the one initially conceived by either of them.

Couples using this creative system recognize that decisions will not be made instantaneously. In fact, some decisions may even be drawn out over a period of months and years. They do not hold to the cynical view that, "A committee is a group of people who began with the intention of creating a horse only to end up creating a camel." These couples assume that a subject is never closed until they come to a point of mutual agreement. Nothing of mutual concern is decided until there is a consensus. Even if one of the spouses comes across with a tone of finality, the other assumes that the matter remains negotiable until they are both satisfied with the decision.[2]

In seeking to implement the syncretic-cooperative system, many couples find it helpful to use a scale from "0" to "10". This scale provides spouses with a way of weighting their opinions. If they feel strongly in favor of something, their opinion has a weight of "10". If they are strongly opposed,

_____

[2]These couples realize there are many objects of great value to man which cannot be obtained by unconnected spouses. An adaptation to consensual decision making is the *quid pro quo* which is suggested by Lederer and Jackson. This is based upon the notion of compromise and involves the giving and the getting of something. A spouse says, "This is my quid—this is what I will give. Now, what is your quo—what will you give?" This is a give and take system in which there is the recognition of a need to compromise. Realizing they will not always be able to arrive at a mutually meaningful and agreeable decision, they agree to let one person have more at one time understanding the other spouse will come out better when a decision is made in another area. The technique enables couples to preserve their dignity and self-esteem.[3]

[3]William W. Lederer and Don D. Jackson, *The Mirages of Marriage,* (New York: W. W. Norton and Co., Inc., 1968), pp. 177-186.

their opinion has a weight of "0". Couples should not make a decision about something until they are at least on the same side of "5". If a husband believes that buying a new car has an importance of "10" and his wife feels that it has an importance of "1", the husband is best advised not to come home with a new car. If the decision about a car is shoved down the throat of his wife, he can be certain that the first time something goes wrong with the car, he will hear, "I told you that car would never hold up!"

By giving a weighting to their opinion, couples get some idea of the difficulty and time that will be involved in making a decision—i.e., if one is at "10" and the other is at "1", they know they have some long discussions ahead of them.

In seeking to resolve conflicts and disagreements, it is sometimes helpful for couples to assess who is going to be hurt the most by a particular type of resolution. For instance, a couple may be faced with making a decision about going to a particular social function, taking a particular type of vacation, or purchasing one item at the expense of another item. In making these decisions, spouses might place pain on a scale from zero to ten. For instance, they may find that if one particular form of resolution is followed that the one spouse experiences a pain to the degree of "10" whereas the other spouse really experiences no pain. Using this method, one would decide upon the solution that would not cause such a degree of pain for the other spouse. For instance, one couple was leaving for a weekend trip. At the same time, their seventeen year old son was also planning to leave for a camping trip. The parents planned to leave immediately after work Friday afternoon, but the seventeen year old was not going to leave until 2:00 in the morning. The father insisted that there was no need to wait for the seventeen year old to leave as he could take care of himself. The mother, however, was uncomfortable leaving before their son, thinking that she would like to help him get on his way. Logically, the husband's opinion that the son was mature and able to take care of himself was right. On the other hand, the anxiety of the mother was very real. In looking at this on the scale from zero to ten, the husband found that it caused him no pain to delay leaving until later in the evening when his wife was more comfortable. The pain experienced by the wife by leaving their son behind was about "8". Within this framework, they were easily able to decide to delay leaving. The husband was able to go along with this without taking any martyr pills as he realized he was not suffering, but that he was cooperating with his wife in finding a solution that was most comfortable for the two of them.

Couples opting for the syncretic system realize there are no easy, right, or correct answers to most of the conundrums faced in marriage. They also realize that neither of them have all of the answers and they are aware that most decisions made by one spouse directly affect the other. In approaching the problem-solving effort, they seek to define the problem, explore it, use a brain-storming method of examining possible solutions, and finally they select a solution with which they can both live. These couples recognize that marital love does not develop simply from doing "nicey-nice" things together. It develops from a realization of the need spouses have for each other. Muzafer Sherif demonstrated this point in the Robber's Cave Study.[4] He conducted a series of field experiments in which groups of boys in a summer camp were organized experimentally and brought into competitive conflict. When intergroup conflict reached a peak, a variety of attempts were made to reestablish intergroup harmony. Of these, the most successful was the arrangement of a task that necessitated the joint effort of otherwise competitive groups.

---

[4]Muzafer Sherif, *et. al., Experimental study of positive and negative intergroup attitudes between experimentally produced groups: Robber's Cave Study.* (Norman, Oklahoma: University of Oklahoma Press, 1954.)

He demonstrated that the establishment of superordinate goals was the most effective means of reducing intergroup conflict. He and his colleagues found that the participation of two groups in competitive activities caused alienation, disharmony, disruption, friction, and discontent. However, only participating in "nicey-nice" camping activities such as roasting hot dogs and watching movies did not effect a feeling of affiliation. The groups developed feelings of affiliation when they were faced with resolving tasks that no one group could resolve completely on their own. The resolution of these tasks effected a feeling of affiliation, cooperation, and harmony. In marriage, we find that a love relation does not develop if spouses compete with each other. On the other hand, love does not develop from simply doing nice things together. Successfully married couples realize that decisions can only be made in a cooperative manner. Furthermore, they realize that a cooperative system aids them in their efforts to develop a meaningful love relationship.

CHAPTER 14

Equal But Different

It has been suggested that marital love emanates from an understanding and awareness of each other in marriage. Along with this, it has also been suggested that a syncretic-cooperative system of decision making is one of the ways in which couples can develop a loving awareness and understanding of the other. This system is based upon a recognition of equality, the acceptance of which enables spouses to enhance and supplement rather than to supplant the dignity of each other. The master-serf relationship which prompted Napoleon Bonaparte to comment that, "woman is given to man to bear children: she is therefore his property, as the tree is the property of the gardener," does not effectively develop a feeling of mutual respect and love. Spouses are separate and distinct individuals who each makes a unique contribution to the viability of the relationship. This is exemplified by:

Creation Of Woman From The Rib Of Man

She was not made of his head to top him;
nor out of his feet to be trampled upon
by him; but out of his side to be equal
with him; under his arm to be protected;
and near his heart to be beloved.

There are psychological and emotional differences between men and women. However, the crucial point is that a difference is not a deficiency. As Oxford physician, Christopher Ounsted puts it, "We are all human beings and in this sense equal. We are not, however, the same."[1]

Marriage may be a less difficult, but also commensurately less rewarding, relationship when it is based upon a master-serf concept. Although it does not build love and respect, it is easier to make decisions when one simply does what he wants and the other follows. Also, the decision making process may have been less complicated when couples operated upon stereotyped notions of sex roles. At the time of our marriage, my wife and I were aware of fairly rigid role expectations. Society offered rather clear distinctions between the role performance expected of a husband and that expected of a wife. Presently, the role expectations are more diffuse. Women have achieved greater freedom and a range of choices far broader than marriage, home, children, and church. In spite of the advantages of this evolutionary process, husbands and wives are more confused about the meaning of their masculinity and femininity. Husbands no longer are so sure that they are figures of authority, the heads of their households. Women receive less respect and protection than was true when the double standard was accepted. Many spouses are struggling to discover the meaning of their masculinity and femininity. Modern couples try to avoid false stereotypes— the "feminine mystique" and the "male mystique." Each spouse is to be treated as a unique person. Ignace Lepp states, "Not so long ago, women were very proud of their mission to be the servants of the species. Today, they are conscious of themselves as persons and desire for themselves all that goes along with being a person; namely, independence, freedom,

---

[1]"Men vs. Woman: Equal—But Different," *Reader's Digest,* (July, 1972), pp. 87-89.

the right to happiness, and the right to individual development. Men have been animated for a long time by the same
desires, but from now on they will not be able to satisfy
these desires except in relation to those of their feminine
companions."[2]

Husbands and wives are unique persons who are equal, but
different, and who relate in a complementary fashion. Although they help fulfill each other and have a mutual dependence, spouses remain uniquely individual. Myron Brenton
explains:

> The most important consideration is not whether most men are
> and do one thing and most women are and do another thing, but
> whether each person of either sex is recognized to be—and en-
> couraged to be—unique unto himself. Society sets up its rules for
> what constitutes masculinity and femininity, but masculinity and
> femininity are, after all, just words whereas human beings are not.
> Too, human beings have an enormous range of possibilities in
> terms of traits and in the ability to play roles of all kinds. These
> possibilities are severely foreshortened by the process of sex
> differentiation too rigidly applied and by masculinity and femi-
> ninity too narrowly defined.[3]

The old stereotypes are difficult for both husbands and
wives. When they have to deny their feelings, husbands become reluctant to discuss anything having to do with their
job, financial worries, hurt feelings, aggravations, hopes,
dreams, and dissatisfactions. They cannot discuss anything
that has to do with their inner self. The stereotypes present
obstacles to becoming aware of the other. One sensitive
husband, unashamed of his feelings, was explaining to me the
difficulty his wife experienced in childbirth. As he dramatically described the pain experienced by his wife, she inter-

---

[2]Ignace Lepp, *The Psychology Of Loving*, (Baltimore: Helicon, 1963), p. 138.

[3]Myron Brenton, *The American Male*, (New York: Coward-McCann, 1966), p.
53.

rupted exclaiming, "Oh, John, it wasn't that bad." John countered, "You didn't have to watch; you don't know how bad it was."

There are many explanations for the evolving concept of equality and the effect it is having upon marriage. I sometimes facetiously wonder if the power lawn mower and the outdoor bar-b-que gave the "greatest impetus" to the process. With the advent of the power lawn mower, wives mow the lawn before their husbands get home freeing the husband to burn dinner on the outdoor bar-b-que.

The concept of equality is confusing in many ways to many couples. Some believe it means they must do everything that is done by the other. They fear their individuality and uniqueness will be lost. Such a fear suggests a distortion of the concept. Equality implies the existence of private thoughts and private dreams. Couples need to develop an appreciation of the private dimensions of their partner's life. They must appreciate that a spouse brings a private self to the shared experience of marriage. Equality and togetherness need not mean that individuality and uniqueness are lost. Some couples operate under the misconception that "they must be one." This illusionary notion suggests that marriage partners can share everything with each other and thus drive out all loneliness and feelings of separation. The spouses believe they gain fulfillment by possessing, and being totally possessed by, the other. Conflicts or attempts at privacy are suspect since they endanger the concept of "everything-that's-mine-is-yours-and-everything-that's-yours-is-mine." Lee and Casebier[4] explain that this attempt to prevent gaps in the marriage ends by creating perhaps the most damaging gap of all, the estrangement resulting from over-possessiveness. They

---

[4]Robert Lee and Marjorie Casebier, *The Spouse Gap,* (Nashville and New York: Abingdon Press, 1971), p. 45.

discuss the risk of being held so tightly that a spouse is squeezed to death in the name of togetherness.

Acceptance of equality is also an acceptance of the concept of accommodation. Spouses face the challenge of developing a multidimensional life. Marriage can be conceived of as a large circle with the spouses being symbolized by two smaller circles contained within the context of the relationship.

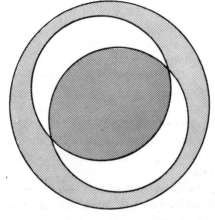

The overlap (shaded area) represents the togetherness of the couple. That is, the dimensions of their life they share. The unshaded area of the two smaller circles is the part that is not totally shared with the other. That may encompass the other vocations of life such as that of employee and citizen. It may also include hobbies such as hunting, fishing, bowling, bridge, etc. It is the involvement in activities which actually contributes to the viability of the marriage but that is not done together. The lined area outside of the two smaller circles represents the life spouses share as a couple with others. This area includes their children, their mutual friends, and other ways in which they share their marital life with other people and institutions such as the church, school, and community. Yet, if spouses place a value upon the marital relationship, it is necessary to guard against moving so far apart that one moves outside the relationship.

Spouses bring their individuality into the marriage and they do live a multidimensional life. The husband may have some interests which exclude his wife and she may have some interests which exclude her husband. The ideal is that these individual interests should serve to create affiliation rather than alienation. As modern spouses pursue their multidimensional life, they must assess whether or not these pursuits are causing affiliation or alienation. There is always the danger that these private interests may alienate spouses from each other. There is the risk of becoming so immersed in doing one's own thing that the marriage suffers. It is possible for one's personal pursuit for fulfillment to damage the marital relationship. If value is placed upon the marriage, the sense of personal fulfillment may itself be damaged if the marital relationship is damaged.

Again, the social scientist must turn to the poet for a meaningful description of togetherness and multidimensional life. In *The Prophet,* Gibran says:

But let there be spaces in your togetherness,
And let the winds of the heavens dance between you.
Love one another, but make not a bond of love:
Let it rather be a moving sea between the shores of
your souls.
Fill each other's cup, but drink not from one cup.
Give one another of your bread, but eat not from the
same loaf.
Sing and dance together and be joyous, but let each of
you be alone,
Even as the strings of a lute are alone though they
quiver with the same music.

Give your hearts, but not into each other's keeping.
For only the hand of Life can contain your hearts.
And stand together yet not too near together;
For the pillars of the temple stand apart,
And the oak tree and the cypress grow not in each
other's shadow.[5]

The other adaptation spouses need to make in coming to grips with the concept of equality is that the differences between men and women are complementary and there is no eleventh commandment which says that there must be "the world of the man and the world of the woman and never the twain shall meet except in the bedroom." My wife and I came to recognize this several years ago while preparing to entertain some friends for dinner. Prior to that time, we had not noticed any change in the ritual of getting up from the dinner table and having the wives do the dishes and talk about womanly matters such as the children and the most effective detergent while the men moved into another room to discuss the very important manly subjects such as sports and politics.

Before the guests arrived, my wife commented that we would be spending the evening with some very strong-willed women. It was not until the next day that we realized the ritual had changed. After dinner, we all went into the living room and talked about various issues such as war and peace, politics, and religion. The wives were as informed as the men. It was not until we were involved in another social situation where the old ritual was practiced that we realized how

----

[5]Quoted from Virginia Satir, *People-making*, (Palo Alto, California: Science and Behavior Books, Inc., 1972), p. 125. She quotes from *The Prophet* by Kahlil Gibran. Copyright 1923 by Kahlil Gibran; renewal copyright, 1959 by Administrators C.T.A. of Kahlil Gibran estate and of Mary E. Gibran. Reprinted by permission from Alfred A. Knopf, Inc.

rewarding was the new ritual in which there was a reciprocal dialogue between the sexes.

In many respects, women are assuming responsibility for the liberal education of the family. Many husbands are involved in a highly technical and specialized world in which they are learning more and more about less and less. Wives are becoming increasingly involved in the macro-scopic issues of politics, social action, and church renewal. If the husband is comfortable with his sense of masculinity, he can be open to learning from his wife. It is the insecure husband who feels that "a woman has her place." This is the old idea that a woman is to be kept pregnant in the summer and barefoot in the winter. No longer are brides admonished, "Your duty is submission. Your husband is, by the laws of God and of man, your superior; do not give him cause to remind you of it." A husband no longer has a legal right to maintain his authority by beating his wife as long as he does not use a stick thicker than his thumb. Marriage is no longer based upon the assumption that the woman is less educated, younger, substantially smaller, or lower in social status.

Equality implies that each person will contribute to the relationship to the maximum extent of his or her ability without having to fit into stereotyped definitions of what constitutes the masculine or feminine role. Each spouse is free to develop his maximum potential unlimited by sex role stereotypes. Within this context, a woman with appropriate talents is free to budget the money of the family, to change the spark plugs on the car, or to crochet. On the other hand, a husband is free to develop his talent as a gourmet cook, raise flowers, or go hunting.

This concept of equality does not imply that there is no leadership within the marriage and that each spouse goes his own way. If the marriage is to be viable, the spouses cannot go off merrily on their own. Equality and freedom demand responsibility and accountability. Equality does mean that the rights of each spouse will be considered when a decision is made. If the "washboard" is broken and a wife asks that they buy a new washing machine, a husband cannot, on the basis of his headship, justify the purchase of an outboard motor rather than an automatic washing machine. Husbands frequently quote only the first part of Paul's advice in Ephesians 5.

> Be subject to one another in the fear of Christ. Let wives be subject to their husbands as to the Lord; because a husband is head of the wife, just as Christ is head of the Church, being Himself Savior of the body. But just as the Church is subject to Christ, so also let wives be to their husbands in all things.

We frequently stop at that point without going on to cite:

> Husbands, love your wives, just as Christ also loved the Church, and delivered Himself up for Her that he might sanctify Her, cleansing Her in the bath of water by means of the Word; in order that he might present to Himself the Church in all Her Glory, not having spot or wrinkle or any such things, but that She might be Holy and without blemish. Even thus ought husbands also to love their wives as their own bodies. He who loves his wife, loves himself. For no one ever hated his own flesh; on the contrary, he nourishes and cherishes it, as Christ also does the Church (because we are members of His body, made from His flesh, and from His bone.) For this cause, a man shall leave his father and mother and cleave to his wife; and the two shall become one flesh. This is a great mystery—I mean in reference to Christ and to the Church. However, let each one of you also love his wife just as he loves himself; and let the wife respect her husband. (Ephesians 5:21-33)

Paul's description of headship deals a demolishing blow to the chauvinist clique.

The Birds[6] distinguish between dominance and domineer-

---

[6] Joseph W. Bird and Lois F. Bird, *The Freedom of Sexual Love*, (Garden City, New York: Doubleday and Co., Inc., 1967), pp. 29-76.

ing, explaining that the latter is autocratic, demanding, and most often a petty tyrant. The dominant husband is not threatened in his masculinity or insecure in his role as husband and father. He, therefore, feels no need to assert his authority. He can freely love others without fearing they will take advantage of him. They also explain that being "subject" to a husband does not mean that a wife is subjugated to him. This role would be wholly incompatible with her nature and opposed to the nature of marriage. They maintain that by fully giving (sharing), a woman attains womanhood. I believe that by fully sharing, a man also attains masculinity.

It is eminently clear that marriage is an intense, demanding, and binding relationship within which one shares his life with all of its hopes, dreams, aspirations, and disappointments. It is a most demanding union which requires spouses to be accepting and understanding of themselves, as well as of their spouse. It demands that they develop a meaningful spiritual life, for without faith in God, the problems of married life would often appear all too frustrating. Without the ability to live by the dictates of the Christian life, with its emphasis upon love, charity, forgiveness and understanding, the problems of marriage become insurmountable.

BIBLIOGRAPHY

Bach, George R., and Wyden, Peter. *The Intimate Enemy: How To Fight Fair In Love and Marriage*. New York: Avon Books, 1968.

> The authors stress the importance of fighting fair explaining that untrained fighting can be dangerous. Under pressure, the temptation is strong to strike at weak points, throw in irrelevancies, and go for a "kill." This book demonstrates, with one hundred and twenty two real fights, the flexible rules and exercises for fair, above-the-belt fighting.

Dalton, Katharina. *The Menstrual Cycle*. New York: Pantheon Books, 1969.

> Dr. Dalton hopes to induce women to appreciate that there is an answer to much of today's unnecessary suffering and men to gain a sympathetic understanding of the problems of the opposite sex.

Girzaitis, Loretta. *Listening, A Response Ability*. Winona, Minnesota: St. Mary's College Press, 1972.

> This book describes the importance of listening to the unique sound of each person.

Lederer, William J., and Jackson, Don D. *The Mirages of Marriage*. New York: W. W. Norton & Co., Inc., 1968.

> A profoundly helpful, incisive analysis of marriage in America. The authors present a systems concept. They deal with the marital relationship as it is.

Powell, John. *Why Am I Afraid To Love?* Chicago: Argus Communications, Inc., 1967.

Reik, Theodor. *Listening With The Third Ear.* New York: Pyramid Books, 1948.

> An intimate and revealing account of the inner experiences of a psychoanalyst by a world famous analyst.

Wyse, Lois. *Love Poems For the Very Married.* Cleveland and New York: World Publishing Co., 1967.

> Mrs. Wyse effectively uses poetry to capture the many dimensions of married life.

Section IV

DISCOVERING INTIMACY

CHAPTER 15

The Ideal

Throughout this book, the reader has been asked to come to grips with various dimensions of the marital relationship. Love, intimacy, and commitment are words to which the reader has become accustomed. The union of husband and wife in the conjugal relationship is not only another manifestation of the couple's union, but it is another way in which couples develop love, share intimacy, and grow in commitment. God has created man in such a way that spouses derive intense pleasure from sharing their *total self* with each other.

There are various ideals husbands and wives try to achieve in the sexual relationship. In this chapter, some of these ideals will be discussed and in following chapters, some explanations will be discussed in an effort to understand why some couples fail to achieve the ideal meaning. Following these explanations, the reader will be asked to explore the role of the sexual relationship in marriage.

One of the purposes of the conjugal relationship is to provide couples with another way in which to say, "I love you." It is also a way for spouses to relieve sexual tension, to fulfill the desire for sexual ecstasy, and to conceive children. It is also recognized that intercourse is not always an expression of love. This act of love can be distorted so as to become an expression of hate or pure exploitation. One of the more common four letter words that refers to intercourse gives the reader an idea of the utter hate which can be expressed through intercourse.

At times, the conjugal act is a fun experience for spouses becoming a part of the play that occurs in marriage. At other times, intercourse may serve as a true validation of one's worth and as a deep expression of acceptance. A mother who has been listening to her young children tell her, "You're not a nice mommy" while her teenagers tell her, "You don't understand a thing" begins, by the end of the day, to believe that she really is not a nice person and not understanding. In a time of despair, intercourse can serve to validate her sense of worth. At these times, intercourse may say, "You are good and wonderful and understanding and lovable." A husband may come home after being laid off from work, uncertain about the prospects of finding another job, and worried about supporting his family. At times like this, a husband has serious doubts about his worth and masculinity. At this time, intercourse says to him that he does not only have extrinsic worth—his worth as a productive commodity—but that he also has intrinsic value. His intrinsic worth is validated in the marriage act where, rather than being expected to produce and perform, he is asked to share his total self with his spouse.

At other times, the conjugal act shows a deep tenderness and intense love for each other. After celebrating their twenty-fifth anniversary and reminiscing about their years together, a couple may join themselves in intercourse rising to the magnificence of love. At these times, spouses recognize the dynamic nature of the sexual relationship. They realize that the honeymoon was only the ticket to begin trying. Although they do not want to detract from the meaning of their initial experiences, they are able to smile at their "amateurish" beginnings and to fully appreciate the dynamic development of their sexual relationship.

It is important for couples to discuss the various meanings of their sexual relationship. Generally, it is easier to talk about something than to do it. However, this is not true with sexuality. Talking about sex is very difficult for many couples, even for those who are intelligent and otherwise articulate. Ironically, married couples find it more difficult to discuss their sex life than they do to live it.

Another meaning of conjugal love is its potential to be representative of a developmental and maturational apex. This is not to mean that man lives by bed alone. However, a truly meaningful sexual relationship makes certain demands upon the spouses that are indices of their maturational development.

For the sexual relationship to be truly meaningful, the lovers must be understanding, accepting, and tender. Are these not the traits we attribute to the truly mature person? Conjugal love can perpetuate these traits because they become more finely developed as we continue to demonstrate them not only in the sexual relationship but in the total life of the marriage.

Conjugal love also serves as a validation of a couple's masculinity and femininity. In spite of the diffuseness of what is specifically masculine and feminine, it remains vitally important that the sexuality of husbands and wives be validated. Both men and women want to believe that their masculinity or femininity are in some way indispensable. It is during the act of intercourse that spouses recognize the dramatic impact of their complementary differences. God has so made husband and wife that they can be joined together in an act which expresses his union with his Church. During intercourse, the husband realizes that nothing is so important to the completion of this act than that he be man. In the same way, the wife realizes that nothing is so important to the fulfillment of this act than that she be woman. It is this phenomenon that causes some to comment that, "All you ever did was make a woman out of me" or "All you ever did was make a man out of me."

In validating each other's sexuality, spouses need to recognize that foreplay does not occur only in the bedroom. Women must be made to feel like women and need to develop a feeling of confidence in themselves and a feeling of knowing they are adequate. Wives are prepared for intercourse by being involved in the total love relationship of marriage and realizing that this relationship brings security, nurturance, and comfort. They are also prepared for intercourse by having a strong conviction that God gave man the potential for enjoying the intense pleasure of sexual relationships. However, for intercourse to be fully meaningful, a woman must feel totally like a woman. If throughout the day, her husband treats her as though she is of very little consequence and good for nothing more than doing "wifely chores," she is not suddenly going to be "turned on" in the bedroom.

In the same way, a husband must feel totally like a man. If throughout the day he is treated as though he is of very little consequence and good for nothing other than bringing home a paycheck and keeping the yard mowed, he is not suddenly going to feel totally sexual and adequate.

This twenty-four hour a day notion of foreplay suggests that intercourse is not something extraneous or optional to marriage. Although it may be the culmination and the symbol of a relationship of self-donation and self-giving to one another, it is a part of the total relationship.

Although many couples attain these ideal dimensions of the sexual relationship, it is also recognized that the sexual relationship, for some husbands and wives, is marred by anxiety, discontent, and perhaps disgust.

CHAPTER 16

How We Learn

The various educative experiences of spouses offer possible explanations for the failure of couples to find the conjugal dimension of their love relationship helpful in their efforts to develop a deep sense of awareness and appreciation of the other. This chapter will examine the effects of repressive and permissive education as well as those of the education provided us as a result of our own personal experiences.

Repressive Education

Soon after I became involved in family life education, I received a telephone call from my mother who explained, "I heard you have been talking about *It* in public. If that's true, I want to know if you are saying the same things that I read about in the paper." When I asked what she had been reading in the paper, she personified the repressive approach by exclaiming, "I wouldn't repeat it over the phone!" Implicit in the repressive approach is the notion that sex is dirty, ishy, awful, bad, and what's more, "nice people really do not talk about it." It is exemplified by the triple terrors of conception, infection, and detection. This limerick puts it quite nicely:

> There was a young lady named Wilde
> Who kept herself quite undefiled

> By thinking of Jesus,
> Social diseases,
> And the fear of having a child.
>
> (Author Unknown)

Many of us can recall and smile at some of the techniques of the repressive approach. The following is a potpourri to which the reader can add some of his own gems.

1. Always kiss through a handkerchief so sexual urges are not aroused.

2. If ever you do have a wet dream, call your parents into the bedroom.

3. Don't walk through water puddles as your underclothing will be reflected.

4. Don't stand over a register or your dress will be blown up.

5. When riding in a car with a boy, keep a bag of potato chips between you.

6. Always wear a rosary around your neck. If the boy still makes advances, give him the peace sign between the eyes.

7. Never wear patent leather shoes as that reflects underclothing.

8. When entertaining a boyfriend for dinner, do not use a white tablecloth as that reminds him of bedsheets.

9. When sitting on the lap of a boy, always keep a telephone book between you.

10. Never touch the dirty parts of your body.

11. A nice girl does not have *those* feelings.

12. Never look in the mirror unless the sinful parts of your body are covered.

Although many people laugh at these bits of advice, there were some unfortunate ramifications of this teaching. Implicit within it was the notion that the sex drive within the man was the size of a set of encyclopedias as compared with the woman in whom the drive was the size of a pocket dictionary. This implication precipitated the double standard of morality which suggests that since the sex drive for the man is such a terribly powerful urge, the young woman is in charge of the depth of sexual involvement. The double standard has given an "out" to many young men who have repeated the familiar refrain: "If she only would have told me in the beginning that she wasn't that kind of a girl. . ." It is also what causes us to look with a jaundiced eye at the girl who is illegitimately pregnant. The contradiction is that we smile rather knowingly at the young man and say, "Well, boys will be boys." It is the same attitude that causes us to ostracize the prostitute, but to smile at the man who uses her services explaining, "Well, you know how it is."

The double standard does not only affect the unmarried. This attitude continues to affect married couples as they struggle with the often agonizing decision of family planning. Two phenomena have made the practice of natural family planning difficult: (1) The double standard prompts the husband to hold his wife responsible for her fertility and causes him to be offended with her if she is fertile at a time that he is passionate. (2) After a couple of martinis, a couple decides they can support the world. We were tempted to nick-name our second child Olive.

Husbands afflicted by the double standard may tell their wives that a decision about a family planning method is up to her. "You go ahead and decide upon whatever you would like to do. As long as it isn't too difficult for me, it will be O.K." The double standard causes men to look upon women as sexual conquests. If control is the responsibility of the woman, victory belongs to the man who breaks down her self-control.

The impact of the double standard struck me during the course of a seminar I conducted in which some of the participants complained to the coordinator about my use of the terms sex and intercourse. They complained that that kind of talk was O.K. when with a group of guys, but not in mixed company. I not only objected to their complaint about my terminology, but if my language was unacceptable in mixed company, it should also be considered uncouth at a stag party.

The above is reminiscent of the 1972 national meeting of the Veterans of Foreign Wars in which the majority of the delegates argued against the admission of women veterans of foreign wars into the organization. One man objecting to the admission of women said, "When I go to a post meeting, I want to say what I want in my own language." Another delegate claimed, "My mother was a lady, and that's better than a man. They should not be put on the same plane."[1] Needless to say, the proposal for admission of women was rejected.

The repressive form of education often uses the words purity and impurity. Joseph and Lois Bird explain that these words, along with others frequently used in reference to sexuality, often lead to an association developed between sexuality and cleanliness and even bodily functions. They refer to this as the "Ivory Soap Concept" of sexuality.

---

[1]*Minneapolis Tribune,* Vol. CVI, No. 91, Wednesday, August 23, 1972, pp. 1A and 11A.

The child hears Mother remark that the baby is 'dirty' and in need of a change; but Mother may also attempt to discourage the child from handling his genitals by employing this same word: 'Mustn't touch yourself there; it's dirty.' The one becomes associated with the other, and the child learns to view the genital organs as dirty or ugly. Consciously or unconsciously, many carry this association into marriage.[2]

We experience the same problem in understanding the biblical statement, "Anyone who looks lustfully at a woman has already committed adultery with her in his thoughts." (Matthew 5:28) This quotation so concerned one woman that she inappropriately applied the concept to married life. She explained that in their ten years of marriage, her husband had never seen her undress. She proudly exclaimed, "I have never given my husband one impure thought." The difficulty in categorizing sexual thoughts as sinful or non-sinful is exemplified by the man who confessed that he had had twenty impure thoughts. The confessor asked, "Did you entertain the thoughts?" The man replied, "No, they entertained me."

One of the purposes of the repressive approach is to help young people control their sexual desires thereby enabling them to delay intercourse until marriage. However, many people have found they could not change their pattern of thinking that quickly. If, in an effort to control sexual expression, one develops the idea that sex is "dirty, ishy, awful, bad," that mode of thinking is not always changed immediately after the exchange of marriage vows. I often think of the girls in our class for whom St. Agnes was established as the epitome of virtue. They were told that as a result of her refusal to let the Roman soldier caress her

---

[2]Joseph W. Bird and Lois W. Bird, *The Freedom of Sexual Love*, (Garden City, New York: Doubleday and Co., Inc., 1967), p. 43.

breasts, the soldiers burned her breasts with hot coals. I wonder how this affects the girls in their adult married life when, during foreplay, they think of St. Agnes.

Many couples who were married when the repressive approach was in vogue can recall the marriage instruction given them by their clergyman. They may have waited for weeks for him to discuss sexuality. Finally, after the wedding rehearsal, the clergyman asks them to come to the parsonage. He then explains that he wants them to arrive at the church a half hour before the wedding and that immediately after the ceremony they should come to the parsonage with their witnesses and sign the appropriate forms. As they are going out the door, he puts his hand on the shoulder of the man and says, "By the way, Tom, whatever was wrong up until now will be O.K. after tomorrow."

Unfortunately for many couples, everything was not all right after tomorrow. Earlier experiences are indelibly recorded in our brain. Our computers are activated by certain stimuli and we re-experience the emotional impact of those earlier experiences. For many, marriage has been the stimulus to activate the computer and to recall the earlier repressive teaching. Many married couples have failed to realize that, "now it is all right." Those who have been programmed to believe that sexual activity is immoral and animalistic, even though that negative guidance was consciously aimed only at instilling sexual self-control in the unmarried state, find it difficult to surrender overnight a sense of guilt or fear. One does not rid himself that easily of repressive injunctions.

As a result of the way in which the double standard of morality was conveyed, many women have been more adversely affected by repressive education than have men. The dictionary versus encyclopedia idea conveys the notion that the man is like an Eveready battery—you press a button and he turns on. On the other hand, the notion is that a woman is to be like an old-fashioned telephone. You grind and grind to get a response. This is a gross misunderstanding which causes us to expect far too much of a man and far too little of a woman. It is interesting that so much information about sex is stored in women and yet it is taught by men. This double standard has placed many wives in a pathetic conflict situation. They were taught that "by nature" they had less sexual drive than a man, were less passionate, less frequently and intensely aroused, and they may have even been taught that sexual desire and satisfaction was not part of their nature. It was implied that a woman should not be surprised if she were frigid. In fact, frigidity may even have been considered virtuous.

The conflict arises when wives discover their capacity to enjoy deep sexual satisfaction and the commensurate rise in their sexual desires. If she becomes concerned that these aroused feelings are "unnatural" she begins to fear that she is not being feminine. Also, this causes many women to fear indulging freely, spontaneously, and fully their sexual impulses with a loving marital partner fearing he might be critical or suspicious or even that he might ridicule such "uncontrolled passion."

A related effect of the Eveready battery versus the crank-type telephone notion is that many wives are basically accepting of the full potential of their femininity, but they look upon intercourse as a beautiful and precious gift which they *give* to their husbands. However, many modern day husbands are concerned that a reciprocal pleasure be derived from the marriage act. Husbands do not want this to be a one-way street in which their wives are the *givers* and they are the *takers*. Rather than to look upon intercourse as something a wife gives her husband, it should be looked upon as something shared together. The gift idea can unfortunately lead to a situation in which a husband believes that intercourse is his reward for good behavior. This concept also fails to emphasize the potential the woman has for fully participating in, and enjoying, the sexual experience. This is a remnant of the old repressive idea that intercourse was the wife's obligation.

The repressive educators referred to "rendering the debt." This gives the impression that wives are martyrs chained to the stake. Years ago, there was theological debate as to how sore a wife's back had to be before she could refuse to render the debt. This caused many wives to develop a ritual of excuses for avoiding intercourse. One of these wives confessed that twice she had pretended she was asleep when her husband approached her for intercourse. The confessor explained that intercourse was not an obligation, but was an opportunity for her to participate in the love relationship of marriage. He sought to help her understand the reciprocal nature of conjugal love. He concluded by explaining that he did not want her to think in terms of a penance, but he did want her to initiate intercourse on two occasions to compensate for having pretended she was asleep. For the first time in her life, she realized that intercourse was a reciprocal relationship which could be enjoyable for her. She telephoned the confessor early the next morning exclaiming, "I'm halfway through my penance and I will finish the rest tonight."

It is also necessary to recognize that the sexual drive of many men was inhibited by the repressive approach. Many a wife has tearfully explained that she was so happy while dating her husband because he made very few sexual advances and had the highest regard for her virginity. However, she adds, "We've now been married five years, and I wish he would make an advance!" Spouses adversely affected by the repressive approach need to recall that the obligation in marriage is to love. The Birds explain:

> In the sexual embrace, this is expressed by attempting to fully meet the needs and desires of the other; that is, by continually

striving to increase the other's enjoyment and satisfaction. This is the giving of self; and it is this giving which transforms the sexual act into sexual love. The obligation in marriage is twofold: To give sexual fulfillment, and to strive to achieve it.[3]

Permissive Education

During my early years as a marriage and family counselor, I saw many husbands and wives who had been adversely affected by the repressive approach. I was frequently angered as I learned what they had been taught. I fervently believed that we needed a new approach that allowed people to fully appreciate their sexuality. Although I favored a more open approach to sex education (formerly known as *It* education), I presently see the need for a system that strikes a balance between the old repressive and the Hedonistically oriented permissive approachs. All of organized religion and specifically the apostle Paul and the theologian Augustine cannot be blamed for the effects of repressivism. Paul taught at a particular time when the meaning of sexuality was being grossly distorted and people were being abused and debased in the name of pleasure. Although Augustine's later views about sexuality were no doubt a reaction to his earlier promiscuous life, it must also be remembered that he wrote at a time during which there was a limited knowledge about human sexuality. It was believed that the sperm contained the full capacity for the development of human life and that women were simply repositories in which the sperm developed to the point of birth. The fertilization of the ovum by the sperm was unknown. As I witness the effects of permissivism, I become increasingly convinced of the necessity of placing into perspective what Scripture says about sexuality as well as the need for developing a pervasive theolog-

[3]Bird and Bird, *op. cit.*, pp. 52-53.

ical view of sexuality. William Graham Cole[4] discusses all major Old and New Testament incidents, attitudes, and precepts involving sex and love.

As one reads this and related books, he realizes that Hugh Heffner's Playboy Philosophy can in no way compete with a scriptural and theological view of sexuality. I prefer the old scriptural translations which state that, "Adam went in unto Eve and knew her." (Genesis 4:1) This statement gives us an idea of the meaning God intended for intercourse. Knowing, in the Old Testament sense, means intercourse and implies a total awareness of the other. It is a psychological, spiritual, and physical knowledge of one's spouse. The Playboy-Hedonistic Philosophy that "anything is all right as long as nobody is hurt," cannot compete with the Judeo-Christian tradition that "nothing is right unless somebody is helped." In the Judeo-Christian tradition, the relationship of man and woman—sexual love—is symbolic of the relationship between God and man. No Hedonistic poet can compete with the philosophical underpinning contained in the Judeo-Christian Song of Songs. Eugene Kennedy quotes:

> In it, the lover finds his world and his beloved. She is his vineyard whose breasts are as walls with towers, whose eyes are like doves, while her hair is like a flock of goats and her teeth like washed ewes; her lips are like scalloped thread, her temple is like pomegranates, her neck like the tower of David, the curves of her thighs like links of a chain, and her belly like a heap of wheat set among lilies. The lover embraces his beloved and thinks of taking hold of the branches of a tree as he discovers in her breasts clusters of the vine and in her breath the odor of apples.[5]

Many of us are beginning to realize that in seeking to correct for the adverse effects of the repressive approach, it

---

[4]William Graham Cole, *Sex and Love and the Bible*, (New York: Association Press, 1959).

[5]Eugene C. Kennedy, *The New Sexuality: Myths, Fables, and Hang-ups*, (Garden City, New York: Doubleday and Co., Inc., 1972), p. 47.

was unnecessary to adopt a "permissive" approach. All that is necessary is to place a contemporary theological view into a perspective consistent with the ageless and timeless Judeo-Christian tradition.

This tradition provides us with the fine line between rigid, repressive moralistic control and loose, irresponsible abandon. In its truest sense, this tradition celebrates sexuality. Sex is not a specific act, but a continuing joyful acceptance of being sexual and the concern to experience and express it in ways beneficial to the individual, the spouse, the contemporary community, and the Kingdom.

Organized religion has only become repressive in its approach as a reaction against the abuses of a pagan society. The permissive approach is representative of the Neo-Paganistic Age in which we are living. The permissive approach is exemplified by the cartoon depicting a man and woman in bed together. The man is saying, "Let's not talk about love at a time like this." The underlying idea is that sex and love are separate and bringing such phenomena as love and commitment into a sexual relationship interferes with the fun. Sex is fun, orgasms are pleasurable, and one ought to have as much sex and as many orgasms as possible with as many playmates as one has the physical stamina to tolerate. This is contrary to the Judeo-Christian tradition which stresses the intertwining of love, sex, and commitment.

The permissives are also great believers in "push-button" sex. If sex partners know the proper technique and what buttons to push, the ecstatic pleasure of orgasm is theirs. I frequently suggest that couples who do not have Ph.D.'s in gymnastics not try to follow the how-to-do-it manuals. This preoccupation with push-button sex and the concentration upon orgasm causes couples to lose sight of the value of relating. Intercourse becomes a proficiency test which is an arduous task rather than a warm, reassuring, and consensually validating experience. Many couples, who fear memory lapses, have literally taken the instructions to bed with them.

Other couples have gotten up after intercourse in order to check the manual and grade their proficiency.

Whereas the repressive approach inculcated feelings of guilt, the permissive approach inculcates feelings of inadequacy. Permissiveness has done nothing to reduce the sexual problems experienced by the married and the unmarried alike. When I advocated a change from the repressive approach, I was certain that a greater degree of openness would relieve people of "sexual hang-ups." I now see as many couples with hang-ups and many whose hang-ups have been traded in for feelings of inadequacy. As a result of the effect of permissiveness, I have become more measured and reserved in making a plea for openness. I feel like the philosopher, George Santayana, who was revising a book after several years. When asked what he was saying differently, he replied, "I have much the same to say, but in a different tone of voice."

Sexual problems today differ from those in the past. Formerly, brides often did not know what to expect from sex. Now, both brides and grooms may expect too much. With all of the sophistication of moderns, couples have gained the impression that sexual responsiveness is the most important thing in their whole marriage. If the wife does not have immediate, intense, and frequent ecstasy in their closest contact, she and her husband become baffled and frightened. The couple wonder if the wife is frigid, if the husband is impotent, if their situation is hopeless, or if they are so mismatched that they should divorce.

If anything, the feelings of inadequacy inculcated by the permissive approach have intensified the problems experienced by people. My colleagues and I have noted that the incidences of frigidity are as pervasive as they were ten years ago and that the incidences of impotence seem to be increasing. We must recognize that this is an observation and not a documented fact. We believe frigidity and impotence are now precipitated by feelings of inadequacy rather than guilt. Of course, many other factors must be taken into consideration in seeking to understand the clinical phenomenon of frigidity and impotence.[6]

I have talked with many young men and women who have been immersed in the free love movement. They have discovered that love is not free. They explain they have paid a terrible price for this as they now struggle with a desperate feeling of hanging loose. Sex means nothing, people mean nothing, and they mean nothing to themselves. Whereas before they believed that hanging loose was a virtue, they now realize they have nothing *to hang onto*. Many college students have explained that many of their friends who advocate sexism would be open to developing a concept of sexuality that encompassed its totality and captured the notion that sex is something we are rather than something we do. These sincere young people believe that many of their friends are desperately searching for a philosophy which has a value orientation beyond that of "fun and pleasure are good."

Ten years ago, I saw many people who were overwhelmed with guilt feelings associated with masturbation. Some of these individuals may have been taught that if one masturbated, he would go blind. For the sexual anarchist, masturbation is an art which one seeks to develop. The "liberated woman" does not need a man. All she needs is her friendly vibrator. Women are advised to get double duty out of their automatic washing machines by standing against them for masturbatory stimulation while getting the day's wash out of the way. Many people feel inadequate because masturbation fails to "turn them on." Since their experience is different from that dictated by the anarchist, they wonder what is wrong with them. It does not seem to occur to them that the

---

[6]The books by Hastings and Masters and Johnson listed in the bibliography will be helpful to the reader who is interested in more information regarding sexual problems.

premises of the philosophy they are following may be out of joint.

There are others who do not talk so much about masturbation as pleasure-seeking, but simply as an opportunity for sexual release. I become concerned when many of my colleagues, who are equally convinced that God is on *their* side, suggest that young men should be encouraged to masturbate before going on a date. This practice is designed to reduce sexual tension and the desire for premarital intercourse which may lead to pregnancy. The radical Glide Methodist Church group from San Francisco has used a pseudo-theological perspective in order to dupe participants in their workshops into believing that most sexual hang-ups are inculcated as a result of misdirected moralistic teaching. They also pretend to provide participants with the means for ridding themselves of their hang-ups. It is believed that if one watches enough stag films (presented under the guise of educational materials), the hang-ups will be dissipated in about forty-eight hours. One appreciates the feelings of desperation gripping many people when it is realized that many prestigious groups, schools, and professional associations have adapted this approach in an effort to *free* people of their hang-ups.

Even David Reuben, author of *Everything You Always Wanted To Know About Sex* and considered by many to be the "high priest" of sex, conveys himself in a mechanistic and push-button manner. It must be admitted that his books have been helpful to many couples. However, I take umbrage with the underlying "sex is a big charge" philosophy. Perhaps Eugene Kennedy touches upon the reason people become susceptible to the permissive philosophy. He explains that sexual experience may become important because, for many people, it is the most meaningful natural reality left in the world of steel and calculation. For many, it is the last touch with nature. Some become desperate about sexual expression because they sense that if they lose this, they may lose the experience of what it means to feel like a human being.

In reviewing David Reuben's book, Robert R. Bell[7] of Temple University cites the need for a book that combines a body of scientific knowledge about sexual behavior with a presentation that would make the reading a positive learning experience. He explains that Reuben's is not the book that fulfills these criteria. "Reuben's book has had great success in the marketplace because it was produced and merchandized as a product. It has all the character and originality of a new brand of underarm deodorant. The style and presentation were carefully worked out to sell the book and vascillates between that of an uptight scoutmaster and a dirty old man." Bell contends that Reuben is often factually wrong explaining "some of his statements are just plain stupid." Bell believes, as do I, that it is sad that thousands of people will take the book seriously because they want information and want to make changes in their life. Bell, who has devoted much of his professional life to studying sexual behavior, finds the book insulting to professionals and even more so to the general public who have been conned into buying it.

Personal Experiences

The effect of either a repressive or permissive approach is relatively negligible compared to the impact of the personal experiences each individual has with the phenomenon of his sexuality. For the vast majority of the population, the exposure to a repressive education has not been irreversibly damaging. Most spouses have managed to brush aside the ludicrous notions contained within this approach and to properly

---

[7]Robert R. Bell, *Journal of Marriage and the Family,* Volume 34, No. 1, (February, 1972), p. 179.

integrate the true meaning of sexuality. Many responsible people simply smile at the permissive approach expressing sympathy for those who fall prey to the absurd philosophy of the sexists. Perhaps it is because our sexuality touches so very deeply the depths of our humanity that it is difficult to successfully develop programs in sex education. Whether we complain that they are simply plumbing courses or that they are too lofty and spiritual, the problem encountered in sex education is that the experience of being sexual is deeply personal.

Sexuality is the very sense we have of being masculine or feminine. A colleague of mine was on-board ship when the captain announced that an iceberg had been sighted. He reassured the passengers that there was no cause for concern as their radar equipment enabled them to safely maneuver around the iceberg. As my colleague stood gazing at the iceberg along with all the other passengers, it struck him that an iceberg was something like human sexuality. The vast mountain of ice lies beneath the surface. He believed it was the same with sexuality. The physical sensation of being sexual is only one tenth of the meaning. The intensely deep meaning lies beneath the surface. That is, the psychological and spiritual ramifications of being sexual. It is this vast mountain of meaning that has a tremendous impact.

Children are wonderfully and delightfully naive about sex. No question is considered foolish by the child and his questions about the birth process, his body parts, and his body functions are no different than his questions about electricity getting into the light bulb and water coming out of the pipe. As a young child, he has not yet learned to be ashamed and has not yet been hurt by being sexual. When one of our sons was four years old, he refused to do something I asked of him explaining that I was not his boss. When I asked him who was his boss, he explained, "Mommy's my boss! I came out of her womb and you didn't have anything to do with it." Although he was missing an essential piece of factual data, this statement was no different than saying he didn't want to go outside in the cold.

However, by the time he is ten or eleven, a child's perception of himself and his sexuality begins to change. An eleven year old boy may be showering in the school locker room when he glances around and notices that not everybody is equal. He recognizes that one boy has pubic hair, that another boy's genitalia are larger, and he glances down at himself thinking that he would give away his new bike in exchange for a fig leaf—even a very small one. Thus begins a very definite consciousness about one's sexuality.

A girl may glance around the locker room noticing that her breasts are not as fully developed as are those of her contemporaries. One ninth grade girl, who had a younger sister whose breasts were more fully developed, came home to her mother complaining, "I'm the only girl in the ninth grade wearing hand-me-up bras." As a result of their self-consciousness, pre-teenagers begin demanding more privacy. Their sensitivities are on the surface and easily hurt. One boy came home after touring a seminary where they were able to go for a swim in the seminary pool. He explained to his mother, "It was so nice, when we showered, no one even laughed."

The feelings developing young men and women have about their attractiveness to the opposite sex affect their perception of themselves and the degree to which they successfully integrate their sense of sexuality into their total perception of self. There are many confusing life experiences the young person must integrate. Responsible parents help their children understand that the pressure of evolving sexual feelings may cause a young man to use love in order to get sex and cause a young girl to use sex in order to get love. The effort to understand the meaning sex has to men and women is one of the tasks to be accomplished in marriage.

To some extent, we can be educated to properly understand the effects of a repressive or permissive educative experience. It is much more difficult to place our traumatic personal experiences into a perspective which allows us to develop an appreciation for our sexuality. This is required if we are to truly have the experience of knowing our spouse.

Also, it must be recognized that in spite of the most sophisticated and comprehensive sex education programs and in spite of the most arduous attention to one's emotional development, an understanding and integration of one's sexuality will not come easily. After the fall in the Garden of Eden, one of Adam and Eve's first reactions was to cover themselves. They were suddenly as conscious of their sexuality as is the seventh grader in the shower room. They were now ashamed and embarrassed. Since the fall, it has not only been necessary to do servile work in order to survive, but it has also been necessary to work at understanding one's personhood of which sexuality is a part.

Many spouses have found it helpful to discuss the extent to which their education in sexuality was affected by repressive and permissive influences. Following this, it is helpful for couples to discuss their personal experiences, again, seeking to understand the effect these have upon their perception of themselves as sexual beings.

CHAPTER 17

Sexual Expression In Marriage

As couples seek to attain the ideal goals and purposes of the sexual relationship, it is necessary to come to grips with some pragmatic dimensions of conjugal love. To this point, it has been suggested that spouses discuss the effect educative experiences and philosophical concepts have upon their personal feelings toward sexuality as well as their sexual adjustment. This chapter will review some practical considerations with which spouses need to concern themselves as they strive toward achieving a deeply profound love experience.

After Thirty

Older spouses (those over thirty) are often prone to believe what the younger generation seems to be telling them about sex. That is, that sex was invented by and intended for the young and vigorous. This bias is exemplified by the retired couple who were shopping in the local supermarket. The wife stopped at a magazine stand, studied the display, pulled out a magazine, and put it in her basket. A few moments later, she returned to the stand and replaced the magazine. The husband said, "Didn't you want to buy that?" "Not now," she replied. "I was intrigued with the title, 'Sex In The 70's,' but then it dawned on me they meant the 1970's."

Men in their forties sometimes comment, "Well, I just

don't have it the way I used to. I'm getting up there in years and don't have the adrenalin or vitality I had when I was young." Frequently this is not so much a biological as a psychological phenomenon. Husbands run headlong into the cultural bias which dictates that "middle-aged" people should not have all that much interest in sex and what's more, they really don't "have it" any more. This risky thinking has severe ramifications for marriage. It is about this time that children are being released from the nest or at least taking a greater responsibility for their own care. For the first time in twenty years, a wife may have some breathing room. As a result of new vigor and a fresh outlook upon life, she may develop a new interest in the sexual dimension of their marriage. Just about the time many wives have an opportunity to be interested in their sexual adjustment, some husbands begin to think they are worn out. The sexual adjustment made by the husband in his forties will possibly determine what his adjustment will be like for the remainder of his life. At this point in his life, he is very involved in work and other activities and he may neglect his wife's concern about the sexual adjustment.

Menopause and Climacteric: There are cultural biases which dictate that a woman will no longer be interested in sex after experiencing her menopause. The cultural biases also dictate that this will be a tumultuous period during which it will be impossible to get along with her. "She must be going through her change" is a frequently fallacious comment which covers a multitude of explanations for difficulties in marriage. The thirty-five year old woman for whom menopause is said to be the cause of her problems is apparently experiencing an early menopause whereas the fifty-five year old woman is experiencing a prolonged menopause.

For most women, menopause need not be a severely traumatic experience and the effects of it need not be irreversible. The physical symptoms experienced during menopause are not all psychosomatic. There are physiological explanations for the hot flashes, nervousness, fatigue, insomnia, general aches and pains, and the headaches. During the six months or so that these symptoms are pronounced, it is necessary for her husband and other family members to be understanding and comforting.

The menopause need not adversely affect a woman's sexual desires. Once completed, a woman may feel that she has, indeed, experienced a change. At this point, she may find she is free of many of the responsibilities of child bearing and rearing and may be able to pursue a long-delayed vocational or avocational interest. She may develop several new dimensions to her life.

The physiological changes for the woman are similar to those which will later be described for the man. Vaginal lubrication is delayed and sometimes diminished. As a result, a woman's physician may suggest a lubricating jelly. The expansive potential of the vagina is reduced, the orgasmic phase of response may be shortened, and uterine contractions may become spastic rather than regular which occasionally may produce pain. Many, if not all of these changes, are reversible by hormonal replacement therapy.[1] Another problem experienced by the woman is thinning of the vaginal wall so that thrusting movements of the penis irritate the adjacent bladder. This may be minimized by adequate lubrication and early ejaculation, but the wife is liable to need a post-coital trip to the bathroom.

If there has been a previous concern about pregnancy, she need no longer worry about this. Although age may affect one's energy level, there is no reason why the sexual relationship cannot assume even more meaningful proportions than

---

[1]Robert C. Kolodny, "Observations on New Masters and Johnson Report," *Medical Aspects of Human Sexuality,* July, 1970, pp. 59-60.

previously experienced by the couple. Those who have never realized the bliss and pleasure for which nature gave them the organs can take advantage of this change in life to explore the ecstasy of married love.[2]

Men also experience a climacteric or a "change in life." This usually occurs at a later age than does the menopause for women. It is characterized chiefly by declining function of the testes and by emotional and psychological concerns. It is part of the process of aging. Men who have heavy responsibilities and live under great nervous tension and physical strain are more likely to develop symptoms than those who take life easy and never seem affected by the passing years. The onset of climacteric, if coped with effectively, need not adversely affect a husband's appreciation of his conjugal relationship. For the man over fifty, the erective response is not eliminated, but merely slowed, and it may take minutes rather than seconds. In addition, the quality of the erection may be noticeably less than during younger years. Also, the volume of the ejaculate is reduced and the force of ejaculation is normally diminished. Several studies have shown that the sexual dimension of marriage continues to be meaningful for couples well into their seventies.

Sex In The 70's: The ongoing interest in the sexual relationship is demonstrated by the sixty-five year old woman who complained to a marriage counselor that her husband

---

[2]A word should also be mentioned about hysterectomies. It is not uncommon for a woman in her forties to have a hysterectomy. Although this need not adversely affect the couple's sexual adjustment, some insensitive husbands, who are ignorant of the facts, complain to their wives: "What good are you now with half your parts missing!"

We frequently refer to the depression experienced by women after a hysterectomy. It should be recognized that the husband is often angry about and disillusioned by the hysterectomy. The depression of the wife is frequently caused by the husband's rejection of her. Many wives can cope with the hysterectomy, but not with the feelings of their husband.

was not being faithful to his marriage vows—that is, he was not giving of himself sexually the way he was supposed to. The alert counselor asked when she first realized this and she complained, "Both last night and this morning." There is no age limit beyond which sex is universally impossible. However, both sexes avoid strenuous activity as they get older not so much because they are incapable as because they are lazy or fearful. Several authors have written about the sexual relationship for both middle-aged and elderly couples.[3]

Extramarital Affairs: I choose to discuss extramarital affairs within the context of aging because I find extramarital involvement frequently to be a function of age. It is not only the young "free-swingers" who have a corner on the adultery market. Various therapists have different experiences and various research studies arrive at different conclusions. However, I find that extramarital affairs occur at two very critical points in life: (1) At the time of a business or vocational crisis, and (2) When a spouse becomes concerned about his own sense of sexual adequacy.

One's sense of adequacy is affected by business and vocational success as well as by confidence in one's sexual relationship. When either of these become threatened, a spouse becomes a candidate for an extramarital affair. The individual experiencing a business or vocational crisis may turn to an extramarital affair to prove that "I really am adequate." It is obvious that the spouse who doubts his or her adequacy as a conjugal mate may turn to an extramarital affair to gain a sense of adequacy. The effort may also be directed to proving that the sexual problem is really the responsibility of the

---

[3]James A. Peterson, *Married Love In The Middle Years*, (New York: Association Press, 1968). William H. Masters and Virginia E. Johnson, *Human Sexual Inadequacy*, (Boston: Little, Brown, and Co., 1970). Isadore Rubin, *Sexual Life After Sixty*, (New York and London: Basic Books, Inc., 1965).

other spouse. The behavior of the adulterous spouse is saying, "Look at me, I get along fine in sexual relationships with others, the problem must be the fault of my spouse."

I am frequently reminded of the admonishment of Pope Pius XII to beware of creeping infidelity. This term directs itself to a problem frequently seen in marriage. Time and time again, spouses involved in extramarital affairs have exclaimed, "If six months ago you would have told me this would happen to me, I would have said you were nuts." Couples need to jealously guard the exclusiveness of their relationship realizing that marriage cannot tolerate a third partner. Many people do not start off thinking they will become involved in an affair. They often say, "I thought our relationship was platonic." In the end, they are shocked and disappointed realizing they have a responsibility to the extramarital partner as well as to their spouse and family. Couples should not be too confident that they cannot become involved in an extramarital affair. They should, indeed, be aware of the prospect of creeping infidelity. Many a dedicated husband or wife has become involved in an extramarital affair thinking he or she was only trying to be helpful to a friend. Too frequently, the helping, platonically-based relationship develops into an intimate sexual encounter from which the partners have great difficulty extricating themselves.

Extramarital affairs frequently develop from work relationships. In the work situation, colleagues spend a great deal of time together and share a very important dimension of their life. The time and sharing factor often leads to the development of a love relationship. An individual can experience rapid alterations from one love object to another. This alteration of feeling from one's spouse to one's "lover" plays havoc with one's marriage and emotional life. Although it seems that one can experience love feelings for more than one person at a time, the love of a person requires an emotional response which exclusively eliminates another object or person except when the love is an intellectualized and not a sexualized object. For instance, one can love his mother, wife, and daughter at the same time, but not if there are erotic components consciously occurring. What one finds is that "two loves" do not make for a right marriage. Therefore, a person must be cautiously guarded in heterosexual work relationships.

Couples also need to be alert to the dangers of "super-cool" parlor games. Many of these are only foreplay games in which the primary purpose is to be sexually stimulated. What starts off as "innocent fun" often leads to severe marital arguments and to a rupture of the relationship. Spouses may think that inter-spouse kissing and petting is the "in thing" to do at parties. It may be "in," but if one places a premium upon the marital relationship, one must also realize that grave risks are being taken.

The more ludicrous game in which some couples become involved is that of spouse-swapping. This shows total disregard for the sanctity of marriage. Frequently, one of the spouses does not fully consent to this involvement and becomes deeply hurt. Entire groups of friends have been severely hurt as a result of their efforts to be "super-cool." The people I have met who have become involved in this game have frequently been the sexually insecure, the socially rebellious, and those who have wanted to prove how free and untied they were to convention. Also, some naive people are led into wife swapping and extramarital affairs believing that will ultimately improve their marriage. For instance, if one is sexually unresponsive in the marriage, some believe that they will be able to develop responsiveness in an extramarital affair. It is theorized that the ability to respond extramaritally can be transferred to the marital relationship. Others believe that if they find themselves emotionally frustrated in the marriage, the satisfaction gained from an extramarital affair will enable them to function more effectively in the frustrating marriage. Others may find that it is difficult for them to relate and to respond emotionally in the marriage. They believe that if they can respond emotionally in an extramarital affair, this new-found ability can be transferred to the marital relationship.

It cannot be denied that an extramarital affair can have a constructive influence upon some marriages. I am always impressed when I see a couple where one spouse has just informed the other that he or she has been involved in an affair and the aggrieved spouse responds, "Well, we obviously have something wrong with our marriage, let's get this squared away and see what we can do about ourselves." I am impressed with their recognition that this event need not sound the death knell to the marriage and that personal and marital growth can be experienced as a result of the trauma imposed by the extramarital affair. However, I think it is very risky to deliberately become involved in an affair in order to alleviate personal and marital problems.

Planning For Intercourse

One of the more unromantic suggestions I have for couples and one which elicits the most resistance—especially from the engaged—is the notion that couples should plan intercourse. This suggestion is generally countered with the protest that intercourse should be a spontaneously loving experience. Couples seem to believe that after they have shared a beautiful married day, they should fall into each other's arms and experience the fulfillment of conjugal love.

Unfortunately, harsh reality impinges upon the idealized expectations of the couple. The husband leaves for work with his daily dose of martyr pills. In spite of his self-pity, I don't know what he would do if he did not have his job to go to.

His wife may either leave for work or, if she is a full-time homemaker and mother, she is left with her work for the day. All spouses go about the day with the business of doing the nutsy-boltsy things that hold life together. After dinner, the enjoyment of which is drowned out by the wails of children who do not like what Mother has cooked, Mother and Father may sit down to help with homework, piano lessons, go to an Indian guide's meeting, etc. If the couple does not have teenagers, along about ten o'clock they fall exhausted before the television shows and eventually retire. The couple is now faced with the mysterious, magical, and ecstatic moment. They have shared their nitty-gritty moments, their recuperative moments, and they are now prepared to share in the ecstatic pleasure of marriage.

They fall into each other's arms totally enraptured by the magic of the moment, the aroma of each other's bodies, and the ecstasy of love. Their arms intertwine, their lips engage, and z-z-z-z-z-z-z.(snore) The reality of it is that they are too fatigued to engage in intercourse. One of the children may decide to have a nightmare at that time or as one mother complained, "It seems that we spend one-third of our married life with a child in wet diapers sleeping between us." Another mother complained that if a burglar ever came into the house, she would probably get up and take him to the bathroom.

One harried homemaker who agreed that married life often made a satisfying sex life difficult complained that after intercourse she may have to jump up to answer the telephone as it is on its tenth ring, run to the door as the person who had been incessantly knocking is just driving away, or rush to kiss, hug, and "cookie" the kids who have been crying and pounding on the bedroom door.

It is because of the very nature of the marital day that planning for intercourse is far more practical and eventually more romantic. The wise couple may say, "Wednesday is a fairly easy day, we can just pick up some hamburgers for supper, get a babysitter in or let the kids shift for themselves, go out for a walk or a drive together, and perhaps we'll be relaxed and invigorated when we get home. Maybe then we will feel like going to bed." If this sounds like programing intercourse—it is. If it is not programed, the couple gets to bed and the husband is thinking, "It's been about five days since we have had intercourse, but I have to get up about 6:00, I have a tough day tomorrow, and I won't get back to sleep for at least an hour or so. However, if I don't make an advance, she's going to wonder if I've been going out or if there is some other problem." As he makes his initial advance, his loving wife lies beside him thinking, "We haven't had intercourse for several days, it's getting awfully late, I have a hectic day ahead of me, but he already put that article about frigidity out in front of me. Oh, I suppose I better respond." Although it is recognized that spontaneous acts of intercourse after fatiguing days can be invigorating and reassuring, it is also true that fatigue and teenagers are the worst enemies to the development of meaningful conjugal love. In spite of the parents' need for privacy, teenagers seem to go to bed later and get up earlier than the parents. They, along with their younger brothers and sisters, have irritatingly intrusive habits. Many couples have developed a much more relaxed sex life after they put a lock on their bedroom door.

One of the difficulties couples face in planning intercourse is the hang-up that intercourse must occur after 10:30 P.M. and that the lights must be out and the shades drawn. Although no exception is taken with turning out the lights and pulling the shades, I do object to the prejudice that intercourse must occur as the last thing in the day. If anything, that may very well be the worst time of the day. Although there is nothing wrong with morning or afternoon, parents need to become very creative in seeking to find ways to maintain their privacy. One ingenious couple spends many romantic evenings in their camper trailer which is parked in the back of their house.

Many couples find, after years of marriage, that their capacity for enjoying conjugal love has basically been untried. Finally, the grandparents may offer to care for the children, the couple may get away for a couple of days, and discover previously untapped dimensions to their sexual love.

The deep personal investment involved in intercourse sometimes prevents spouses from being so open and direct as to plan these moments. A husband or wife may fear that the other will refuse. Such refusal may be interpreted as rejecting one's total self.

On the other hand, as a result of educative experiences or simple reticence, some spouses have trouble being that direct. Many of these couples have worked out subtle messages such as the wife who asks her husband if he wants her to mow the lawn during the day or to rest and be relaxed that evening. This is her message to him that she is interested in intercourse. He is then free to respond, "Oh, the grass is getting pretty long and I guess it needs to be cut," or "Oh, the grass will wait another day, there's no hurry, why don't you just relax."

Perhaps the argument between the romanticist and the pragmatist is best described by Judith Viorist:

Sex Is Not So Sexy Anymore

I bring the children one more glass of water.
I rub the hormone night cream on my face.
Then after I complete the isometrics,
I greet my husband with a warm embrace.

A vision in my long-sleeved flannel nightgown
And socks (because my feet are always freezing).
Gulping tranquilizers for my nerve ends,
And Triaminic tablets for my wheezing.

Our blue electric blanket's set for toasty.
Our red alarm clock's set at seven-thirty.
I tell him that we owe the grocer plenty.
He tells me that his two best suits are dirty.

Last year I bought him Centaur for his birthday.
(They promised he'd become half-man, half-beast.)
Last year he bought me something black and lacy.
(They promised I'd go mad with lust, at least.)

Instead my rollers clink upon the pillow
And his big toenail scrapes against my skin.
He rises to apply a little Chap Stick.
I ask him to bring back two Bufferin.

Oh somewhere there are lovely little boudoirs
With Porthault sheets and canopies and whips.
He lion-hunts in Africa on weekends.
She measures thirty-three around the hips.

Their eyes engage across the brandy snifters.
He runs his fingers through her Kenneth hair.
The kids are in the other wing with nanny.
The sound of violins is everywhere.

In our house there's the sound of dripping water.
It's raining and he never patched the leak.
He grabs the mop and I get out the bucket.
We both agree to try again next week.[4]

In spite of my endorsement for planning intercourse, I fear the nature of many marital days can be used as cop-outs for falling into the senescence of marriage. Within the Judeo-Christian tradition, couples are free to view each other as

---

[4]Judith Viorst, *It's Hard To Be Hip Over Thirty and Other Tragedies Of Married Life,* (New York: Signet Books, The New American Library, Inc., 1968), p. 63.

playmates, to have fun in their love-making, and to strive to be appealing and attractive to each other. If couples fall into the senescence of marriage, their sex life simply becomes another part of a dull routine. Before going to bed, many wives spend a half-an-hour in the bathroom getting their hair wrapped up in enough tissue so it looks like a cyclone hit the Charmin Tissue Company just as they were driving past. It may look as though they put their night cream on with a trowel. They may then come trudging out in their socks and nightgown and not look the most appealing. Rather than to settle into the old age of marriage, wives can continue to look attractive and to seduce their husbands. One husband complained that he gave his wife a lovely peignoir for their honeymoon. The next time he saw it was five years later when the kids were using it for a Halloween costume.

Husbands also need to work at creating a romantic atmosphere and environment for sexual encounter. Intercourse is a close and intimate expression of love and personal cleanliness is essential. Many wives are sexually turned off simply as a result of their husband's personal habits. If a husband has been fixing up the yard, changing the oil in the car, and cleaning out the garage, he is best advised to shower before he lets the passion of the moment overtake him. During foreplay, a husband caresses the very soft body of his wife. If he earns his living in the construction trades or some other job which causes his hands to be abrasive, it would be best if he stopped at the local drug store and picked up the weekly special on Corn Huskers Lotion.

Joseph and Lois Bird explain:

> Devoid of romance, however, sexual love becomes monotonous, unpleasant, and even exploitative. In other words, it ceases to be love. The wife feels "used" by her husband, resentful of his egocentric approach to sexual relations. One wife bitterly spoke of the unromantic, matter-of-fact manner in which her husband

approached marital relations. As she talked, her frustration erupted in tears and hostility: "Sex? What is it to him? He doesn't love me; I'm just his sleeping pill."[5]

Specific Concerns

There are other matters of concern to couples. Spouses want to be normal in all respects including their sex life. For that reason, they become concerned about mutual climax, the length of intercourse, and the frequency of intercourse.

Orgasm: As a result of an orgasmic orientation and emphasis, many couples become inordinately concerned about their capacity for mutual climax. Modern husbands are frequently overwhelmed with feelings of inadequacy if their wives do not climax each and every time they have intercourse. This high expectation and the commensurate tendency for self-blame appears to be the cause of impotence for many husbands.

In the same vein, wives who have been exposed to the limited philosophy underlying the "sex is fun" attitude feel they are inadequate sex partners if they do not climax during every incidence of intercourse. Also, for many competitive couples, the failure of the wife to climax becomes another fertile ground for conflict. The husband looks askance at his sexually inadequate wife who, in turn, is disdainful of her sexually nonstimulating mate.

During a weekend my wife and I spent in a seminar with engaged couples, we noted the inordinate concern they had about orgasm. Those who had mutually nonorgasmic premarital experiences were concerned as to whether or not they would experience orgasm after marriage. Those who had

---

[5]Joseph and Lois Bird, *The Freedom of Sexual Love,* p. 98.

mutually orgasmic premarital experiences were concerned as to whether or not the quality of the orgasm would be maintained in marriage. Those who had not had premarital intercourse wondered if they should experiment sexually in order to determine whether or not they were sexually compatible.[6]

My wife and I explained that conjugal love was an intimate language of love. We commented that the learning of this language required time, patience, and mutual awareness. We discussed intercourse as a warm and reassuring experience and one that would not always provide the ultimate ecstatic experience. Most of the couples were relieved that they did not have to seek to become sexual performers and to find that they could take the rest of their married life together to learn this language of love.

After the discussion, I asked my wife if she had experienced orgasm the first time we had intercourse. Both of us had to admit that, at that time, we did not know what orgasm meant. It is not unusual for couples to be married for several months before they experience mutual orgasm. Although they become more satisfied with their sexual relationship in time, they do not want to denigrate the meaning of those initial months when they were learning together.

Although couples should be assured that they do not have to judge their sexual adequacy on the basis of the incidence of mutual orgasm, it is also important to caution couples against using this as a cop-out. Perhaps mutual discussion of the meaning of, and approach to, intercourse may help per-

---

[6]The couples who had not caved into the pressure for premarital coitus also wondered if there was something wrong with them. Many of their friends told them they were foolish to wait until marriage and some college professors and clergy advised some of the couples to test their compatibility before marriage. Other than the adverse moral implications, I believe that the premarital sexual experience serves no positive purpose in the later marriage.

plexed couples discover ways in which mutual orgasm could occur with a more meaningful frequency. Although many husbands are over-concerned about the orgasm of their wives, there are still many who view sex as something *men* ought to enjoy. For these men, the pleasure of the wife is a secondary concern. Many wives begin to reach a point of excitation, begin to feel that the sexual experience is rewarding, the husband climaxes, rolls over, and goes to sleep. His frustrated and angry wife may lie beside him thinking that the next time they will have intercourse is when her sister is ordained a priest.[7]

Frequency: Couples who are concerned about the frequency of intercourse should not try to keep up with the Jones—they might be newlyweds. However, many couples fail to recognize that their sexual adjustment is a highly individual matter. The sex life of the neighbors is unimportant. What is important is that the individual couple should find their sexual relationship to be mutually rewarding to them. If the couple who has intercourse once a month is as happy with their sexual relationship as the couple who has intercourse three times a week, the former couple need not beseige themselves with feelings of inadequacy.

One man came to me asking whether or not he was a sex maniac. He explained that he wanted intercourse once a week and that his wife wanted intercourse once a month. His wife believed him to be a sex maniac. He pressured me to give him an exact number of times per month that would indicate whether or not a person was a sex maniac. I explained that the incidence was not nearly as important as the attitude and rationale. Since they disagreed on the desired frequency, they

---

[7]There are several books specifically directed to sexual problems such as impotence, premature ejaculation, frigidity, etc. to which the concerned reader can turn in the event there is need for additional information. These are listed in the bibliography.

definitely had an unsatisfying sexual adjustment. However, the problem was deeper than this. His wife believed that intercourse was a big favor she did for her husband and once a month was often enough to "give *It* to him."

On the other hand, I saw a man who had intercourse thirteen times a day. Now, he had a problem! The indication of the problem was not that he had intercourse thirteen times a day, but that he counted. When something happens more than four or five times, we generally use the expression "many" and do not bother to count to thirteen. The fact that he counted to thirteen suggested that he tried to compensate for feelings of sexual inadequacy and doubts about his own masculinity by having frequent intercourse. He believed that the high frequency of intercourse proved his sexual prowess.

Couples find that the frequency of intercourse depends upon their schedule. An accountant preparing tax returns probably has intercourse a limited number of times between mid-January and mid-April. On the other hand, if he and his wife take a vacation in May, intercourse may occur several times a day.

In one respect, couples ought to be concerned about their frequency of intercourse. Since there is the general tendency to put less time into making our marriage successful than we do into being successful parents or employees, a lack of intercourse may suggest that the couple is being careless about their marriage. The infrequent incidence of intercourse may be indicative of an overall lack of enthusiasm about the marriage.

Also, it is important to stress that there are some couples who have had a severely disturbed sexual adjustment. Although the rest of the marriage was relatively rewarding, their sex live was just too big of a hassle. Because of this, they decide to avoid sexual contact, but to maintain the marriage. Even though it must be recognized that these are not couples

without serious emotional problems, the avoidance of intercourse can be a way in which some couples hold their
marriage together and maintain their emotional equilibrium.

Length of Intercourse: Some misguided spouses grade
their sexual proficiency by the length of time they can
continue intercourse. Some couples prolong intercourse for
two hours believing they are proving themselves more adequate than the average, unliberated couple. It must also be
remembered that many wives are offended when their husbands do not take enough time and when intercourse is
treated as something squeezed in between coming home from
work and eating dinner. One disillusioned wife explained that
her husband took only two minutes from the beginning of
foreplay to reaching his own climax. He would then roll over
and go to sleep, leave for work, or leave for a game of golf.
The offended husband argued that he clocked it the last time
and it took six minutes. Obviously this couple must work out
a sexual relationship that is mutually satisfying rather than
being satisfying to one partner and frustrating to the other.
In reality, many well-adjusted couples find that intercourse,
from the time of foreplay to the completion of the act, takes
about twenty minutes.

Husbands and wives spend many years of their married life
seeking to develop an internalized understanding of masculine and feminine attitudes toward and responses to human
sexuality. It is because of masculine and feminine differences
in attitude and response that the matter of arousal and time
is a source of misunderstanding between spouses.

Frequently, wives comment that they would like to be
able to hold each other and to not always feel that they will
end up in bed. One cannot take issue with this and it is a
statement that husbands should seek to understand. This
does not mean one's wife is totally uninterested in intercourse. It simply means that at a particular point in time

(such as while preparing dinner, getting dressed to go out, or while her parents are sleeping in the next bedroom) she would like to hold her husband and not necessarily have intercourse. What frequently happens is that wives avoid all types of sharing of affection because they fear that any real affection is going to be misinterpreted by the husband as a message that they want to go off to the bedroom. Also, a wife may fear that her husband will become aroused if she shows any affection and that he will want to have intercourse.

On the other hand, there is another danger of couples misunderstanding and misinterpreting each other. Frequently, wives feel that having about fifteen extra minutes and taking advantage of that time for intercourse means that the experience is not all that involved, meaningful, or important. It really becomes a difference in thinking. Rather than to think it can't mean very much if completed in fifteen minutes, a husband might think, "Gee, isn't it nice that we have fifteen minutes to share this experience." In many instances the wife may ask her husband, "Is this all you come home for?" On the other hand, the husband may think, "Isn't it nice that I can come home and we can have a chance to share this experience."

As well as there is the danger of not putting enough meaning into the sexual experience, there is also the danger of failing to recognize that for some people, the experience can be equally meaningful whether there is an hour to be together or fifteen minutes.

Foreplay

In Chapter 15 it was suggested that foreplay did not only occur just prior to intercourse, but that it involved the total marital day and the way in which spouses validated each other's sense of sexuality. In a more specific sense, one can talk about the foreplay which occurs prior to intercourse as preparing the husband and wife for the union of intercourse. It effects a lubrication of the vagina until the couple develops an irresistible desire for coitus. Again, it is important that couples be able to talk with each other in order to help the other understand what primary and secondary erogenous zones are most responsive and what stimulation elicits the greatest pleasure. Although a woman's primary erogenous zones are her lips, nipples, clitoris, and vagina, her whole body is literally an erogenous zone. The ears, throat, nape of the neck, breasts, small of the back, abdomen, buttocks, and inner thigh all are secondary erogenous zones for many women. The husband, motivated by love, can discover the caresses which give his wife the greatest pleasure.

Although many believe that men do not have erogenous zones comparable to women, it is a mistake to conclude that a wife's caresses are not stimulating or pleasurable. Although most men are less responsive than women to nongenital caresses, it is important to caress the genitalia and other body zones the husband identifies as responsive.

During foreplay, a couple may literally cover each other's body with kisses. They prepare each other for penetration. Many couples find that the husband is prepared for penetration before his wife. I used to joke about this phenomenon explaining that by the sixth day, when it was time to create man, God had tired. Thus, because of his fatigue, He created two sexes with sex drives that were not compatible with each other. More lately, I have come to believe that, once again, God was right. If intercourse is designed to reflect the total quality of the marriage as well as to help spouses become more aware of each other enabling them to apply this awareness to the other hours of married life, they would not learn much if they were perfectly compatible. When couples are able to use the conjugal act to become aware of each other's needs and reactions, the lesson learned can be applied to the total marriage. The reciprocal nature of this is appreciated when we realize that the awareness we develop of each other outside of the bedroom can be applied to the sexual expression of our love.

As couples become more aware of each other, they develop the capacity to be more sexually responsive. Increased experience also makes orgasm more regular. It seems that the ability to respond sexually can only be acquired with experience. Because a woman's sexual anatomy is diffuse, the process of learning this language of love is subtle and complex. She learns to relax, to let herself go, and to abandon herself. As this is accomplished, she becomes aware of entirely new sensations. The husband who narcissistically concentrates on his own sensations and fantasies hurries his own orgasm; while the man who concentrates on the reactions of his wife delays orgasm.

Positions For Intercourse

Although the emotional and philosophical position the couple has toward sexuality is more important than their physical position for intercourse, couples should feel free to experiment with various positions with which they are comfortable. However, they need not seek to be physical contortionists. It is advisable to maintain a physical position for intercourse that allows for maximum contact between the sexual triggers—the penis in contact with the clitoris, the chest and breasts touching each other, and the lips in contact. Spouses sometimes become concerned as to whether various means of foreplay or positions for intercourse are morally reprehensible. As long as the primary concept of physical union between husband and wife is maintained, the couple need not be concerned about sinning. However, they can offend the other by being inconsiderate of the other's physical and emotional sensitivities. This offense to the other may be considered morally reprehensible.

Perhaps the most frequent question asked regarding the morality of sexual practices in marriage is whether or not fellatio and cunnilingus are morally acceptable.[8] As long as foreplay culminates with coitus, there is nothing morally wrong about this practice. However, if one or the other spouse is repulsed, the practice is then wrong. Others may argue that the reluctant spouse should learn to appreciate this technique of love-making. That may be true, but the appreciation should not be foisted upon the reluctant spouse.

Husbands and wives may try various positions for intercourse such as the standard one of the husband being on top of the wife with his legs placed inside of hers. This is sometimes uncomfortable for the wife and the couple may exchange with the woman being on top of her husband. It is ludicrous to refer to this as the male superior or male inferior position. Neither position suggests that one or the other is superior, it only suggests that the couple is seeking to find a position for intercourse that is mutually rewarding. For the husband who comes to orgasm before his wife is prepared, the latter position may be desirable as orgasm tends to occur less quickly if the man is under his wife. Couples may also use a side position in which they face each other and the wife places her right or left leg over her husband's thigh. Many couples find that they go through a period of experimentation and then settle upon a position that is most comfortable and pleasurable for them.

The climax for the husband is an ejaculation which is accompanied by a pleasurable experience due to rhythmic

---

[8]Fellatio is the term used to denote the woman kissing the penis and placing it in her mouth. Cunnilingus denotes the act in which the man stimulates the vaginal area with his tongue.

muscular contractions. At the time of ejaculation, he ejects approximately one teaspoon of semen containing one hundred million sperm. The orgasm is a neuromuscular release, i.e., sudden explosion of energy. For the wife, there is no ejaculation similar to that experienced by the man; however, the orgasm is accompanied by a neuromuscular release which is equally satisfying and similar to that experienced by her husband.

Following sexual climax, the loving couple seem to close out the rest of the world and to lie together treasuring the experience they have shared. Although they may not feel like talking at that particular moment, it is important that at some point in time the couple mention to each other the meaning particular sexual experiences have for them. Consistent with the theme of Chapter 8 which discusses the supportive role in marriage, it is wise for couples to thank each other for the experience they have shared together. Some couples who have a deep appreciation of the role God plays in their marriage thank Him for the experience for which He prepared them. If couples fail to discuss the meaning of their conjugal love, they may develop many doubts about what the other is thinking. As was found in Chapter 11, the chances that we will predict erroneously are better than even. Patience and time are required to develop a full appreciation of conjugal love. It is an art which cannot be rushed if it is to retain its quality as an art. Only if it retains an element of timelessness, can the love-making become an artistic creation of beauty. It must be approached with patience, imagination, and the desire to create a sexual union that will reflect the awesome mystery of the vocation to which husband and wife are called. Only then, can it become an art, and only then can it become fully loving.

Mature sexuality can only be achieved through years of strength, love, personal growth, understanding, insight, spiritual acceptance, and peace of mind. In the midst of the sexual crisis discussed earlier in this section, it is reassuring to realize that, in reality, the conjugal experience is a near perfect blending of the two personalities into an almost total love. The total union envisioned by Christ in His "two in one flesh" concept is beautiful and something for which couples can strive. This union can be achieved in union with God because it is a part of His perfection.

BIBLIOGRAPHY

Barclay, William. *Ethics In A Permissive Society*. London: Fontana Books, 1971.

Bird, Joseph, and Bird, Lois. *The Freedom of Sexual Love*. Garden City, New York: Doubleday and Co., Inc., 1967.

This book treats the subject of human sexuality with candor, sensitivity, and sympathy.

Cole, William G. *Sex And Love In The Bible*. New York: Association Press, 1959.

A revealing examination of all of the practices and teachings in the Old and New Testaments. The author examines the relevancy of these teachings for modern man.

Eller, Vernard. *The Sex Manual For Puritans*. New York: Abingdon Press, 1971.

Though the book is all in fun, the reader can see the serious points Eller makes about the old-fashioned joys that can develop from a deep and devoted marriage. Before its over, Eller takes broad swipes at Dr. Reuben, Playboy Magazine, Situation Ethics, The Greening of America, and Woodstock Nation.

Fuchs, Joseph. *Human Values In Christian Morality*. Dublin: Gill and MacMillan, 1970.

Hastings, Donald W. *Sexual Expression In Marriage*. New York: Bantam Books, 1966.

223

Dr. Hastings hopes that this book will help eliminate the trial and error method of sexual learning.

Kennedy, Eugene C. *The New Sexuality, Myths, Fables, and Hang-ups.* Garden City, New York: Doubleday & Company, Inc., 1972.

Kennedy pulls no punches as he exposes the growing crop of new myths and legends surrounding sex and its expectations for what they really are: myths, distortions—which have victimized man by imposing unrealistic goals and thereby heightening his hang-ups, frustrations, anxieties, and feelings of inadequacy.

Lewin, S. A., and Gilmore, John. *Sex After Forty.* New York: Medical Research Press, 1952.

A book of hope for men and women in or nearing the turbulent years.

Masters, William H., and Johnson, Virginia E. *Human Sexual Inadequacy.* Boston: Little, Brown and Co., 1970.

This book adds clinical experience with human sexual function and dysfunction to pre-clinical investigation. Knowledge in both areas provides a solid base from which to construct improved rapid-treatment programs for human sexual inadequacy.

Masters, William H., and Johnson, Virginia E. *Human Sexual Response.* Boston: Little, Brown and Co., 1966.

A major breakthrough in our knowledge of human sexuality.

Packard, Vance. *The Sexual Wilderness.* New York: David McKay Co., Inc., 1968.

The author reveals how chaotic and conflicting are our beliefs and behavior in every respect to male-female relationships.

Peterson, James A. *Married Love In The Middle Years.* New York: Association Press, 1968.

How husband and wife together can discover the richer joys of maturity in sexual fulfillment, family relationships with children and grandparents, personal identity, financial security, physical and psychological well being.

Rubin, Isadore. *Sexual Life After Sixty*. New York: Basic Books, Inc., 1965.

   Demolishes the misconceptions that hinder a full, healthy, and creative-expression sexuality in the later years.

Section V

WILL MARRIAGE SURVIVE?

CHAPTER 18

Where Is Marriage Going?

During the French Revolution, a man ran into a shop and asked, "Which way did the mob go? I must know at once." The shopkeeper asked, "Why do you have to know?" The exhausted man replied, "Because I am their leader."

The modern husband and wife are reminiscent of this leader looking for his mob. Today's couples look perplexed at what is written and said about modern marriage. They wonder whatever happened to those sacred institutions which they thought were beyond challenge. Perhaps one problem of modern man is that he believes too much of what he reads and hears.

The "gloomers" suggest that parents are immigrants to their own country and too insecure, uninformed, and insincere to be relevant forces in the lives of their children. Some commentators suggest that the family system is too archaic to survive. They conclude that twenty-four hour a day nurseries should relieve the modern woman of the yoke of maternal responsibilities.

Some "gloomers" also suggest that the traditional concept of monogamous and immutable marriage is old-fashioned, unrealistic, and a hindrance to the individual's quest for fulfillment. As a result, the person committed to the traditional idea of exclusive and permanent marriage begins to doubt the relevance of his convictions.

Too often, spouses hear only the wails of the professional mourners. The modern spouse needs to reflect calmly on the pressures impinging upon modern marriage. At the same time, he needs to reexamine the relevance of his traditional convictions. This challenge faces the reader with the test of a first-rate intelligence—the ability to hold two opposed ideas in his mind and, at the same time, still retain the ability to function.

From many sectors of society, today's husbands and wives hear clamorings about the changing family, the modern family, and the family of the future. Many of these claims sound the death of traditional marriage, or at least, notify society that traditional marriage is obsolete. The clamorings alert spouses to changes (such as multilateral marriages, trial marriages, communes, etc.) which seem totally alien to the person committed to the sanctity, permanence, and exclusiveness of the marital bond.

I do not deny the existence of options to traditional marriage, or even that people are exercising the options. I do, however, question the desirability of the options. Do the experts and commentators who alert society to the existence of change and crisis do anything to help spouses and parents gain a clear perspective of the impact of these changes?

The "cop-out" of an expert is to remind his listeners that they cannot behead him simply because he is the bearer of bad news. This statement allows many commentators an irresponsible latitude. "Authorities" who accept the reality of new and popular options for marriage help insure the adoption of these options as the norm in present-day society. Most spouses want to be normal; it is understandable that, in order to be considered so, many of them bring their behavior in line with what they are led to believe "everyone else is doing."

In considering some of the modern writing about marriage, I am reminded of Clemenceau's comment that "war has become too serious to leave to the generals." Perhaps this applies to marriage. Has it become too serious to leave to the "experts?"

As spouses digest the warnings or platitudes of experts and commentators and as they view the revolutions that are occurring within the family, they need to realize that many suggestions for change are short on analysis and long on feeling. Many spokesmen tailor their remarks for media intake rather than problem solving. The challenges facing today's couples afford an occasion for dreamers to conjure up utopias of liberated existence that admit to no human limitation.

I do not intend to underestimate the challenges or even the threats facing today's family. The changes and revolutions occurring within society challenge the perseverance, tap the creativity, and test the faith of the most stout and committed spouse.

Rather than be overwhelmed by the dismal predictions of commentators, the modern spouse needs to realize that it is still popular to marry and to be committed to each other for life. The majority of couples are not only faithful to this commitment, but they find reward and fulfillment in their lives together. Today's husbands and wives need to recognize that it is not old-fashioned to be traditional about marriage.[1]

Marriage is more popular than ever. However, the family carries the burden of multiple problems and is changing swiftly. Published literature on marriage and family life evidences a deepening interest in and concern about the family in a time of unique and accelerating change. Even if there is reciprocal relation between person and community as well as between family and society, the family is the

---

[1]The above paragraphs, by the author, were previously published in "Marriage and the Family: A Tradition for the Seventies," *Our Family*, January, 1972, pp. 2-7.

barometer of the nation, in fact, of the whole family of mankind. Therefore, anyone seriously interested in human welfare and the future of man in a changing culture must concern himself with the inner dynamics of family life.

Human knowledge is now doubled every seven years. Information explodes. The United States government alone annually invests more than seventeen billion dollars in that great engine of change: basic research. Consider only the last decade's developments in space, computer science, cybernetics, molecular biology, and the medical sciences, to see how swiftly new knowledge is harnessed in technology; how soon the whole culture is altered; and how swiftly the impact on human and family living is felt.[2]

The fact of a changing attitude and behavior toward marriage is undeniable. The specific cause for the changing attitudes cannot be explained. Some believe that the information explosion or the continual threat of war is responsible for the changing attitudes. Others such as Carle T. Zimmerman believe change is cyclical and to be expected. He states that:

> No social trend continues endless in the same direction.
>
> Since any change in family behavior is the result of a compromise of many forces—individual, ethical-religious and political-structural—its movements are rather slow. In addition, the cycles are irregular. It may take some generations for a family system to reach an extreme position, but once reached, the resultant social anarchy becomes so disruptive that one generation apparently sees most of the effort toward recovery achieved. . . . The demoralization in Russia arising from the changes toward "factual familism" after 1917 prepared the society for the "remoralization" achieved in the family codes of 1936 and 1945. In a large

---

[2]The above two paragraphs, by the author and Paul Marx, were previously published in "Family Life: The Agony and the Ecstasy," *Future of the Family*, (Ed. Clayton C. Barbeau) New York: Bruce Publishing Company, 1971.

sense, this is the probable pathway the American family system may follow.[3]

Albert Szent-Gyorgyi[4] and Alvin Toffler[5] are only two of the many other authors who have addressed themselves to a study of man's effort to fit into his environment.

There are some changes in thought which have occurred in the past generation. All too few realize the extent of the philosophical revolution, the advance of Existentialism, the modern interest in situation or contextual Ethics and the New Morality which many too simply call the "old lust." These changing attitudes have had a marked effect upon marriage and family life.

A premise which undergirds and makes possible these changing attitudes and behaviors is that one cannot make judgments about another. Closely related to this premise is the acceptance of a concept of alternative life styles which includes divorce and remarriage, trial marriage, communal living, etc. These changing attitudes and behaviors are part of several philosophical revolutions which will be examined in the following pages. Before these revolutions are examined, it must be remembered that there is nothing all that new under the sun. The attitudes and behavior presently viewed as contrary to traditional thought and behavior have all been experimented with, argued about, and integrated into the structure of society at various times in history.[6]

---

[3]Carle C. Zimmerman, "The Future of the Family in America," *Journal of Marriage and the Family*, Vol. 34, No. 2, May, 1972, p. 330.

[4]Albert Szent-Gyorgyi, *The Crazy Ape*, (New York: Grosset and Dunlap, 1970).

[5]Alvin Toffler, *Future Shock*, (New York: Random House, 1970).

[6]This comment was documented by Phillippe Garigue, President of the International Union of Family Organization in a paper entitled "Welfare and the Future of the Family" which was presented at the October 30, 1970 meeting of the American Association of Marriage and Family Counselors in Philadelphia, Pennsylvania.

I'm Free Of Hang-ups

This statement typifies the shallow goal of the liberated existence which is a fundamental part of the modern philosophical revolution in which its participants want to be free of hang-ups related to marriage, life style, and sexuality. Many people explain that they have no hang-ups about sex. They then protest that they can have sex with anyone and not feel any pangs of guilt about it. Someone else will talk about his marriage and his extramarital affair, explaining that he really has no hang-ups about marriage and there would be no pangs of conscience about getting a divorce. Another individual may simply talk about the matter of marital fidelity explaining that he has no hang-ups about monogamy and adultery. Someone else may talk about responsibility to his family or children. This liberated individual may proudly explain that he has no hang-ups about neglecting his family or children or placing them in second place to a career, social life, or an extramarital affair. After all, "the rights and happiness of the individual are of primary importance!" Adherents to this philosophy have no compunction about putting themselves first and placing secondary importance upon other responsibilities. They operate upon the notion that "after me, you come first."

I have often thought that the people who say they have no hang-ups "protest too much." They explain they want to "hang loose," be freed of traditional values, and be open to various options in life. As they talk, one finds that they have been divorced and that they have had several jobs in the past few years. These phenomena are indications of the new-found freedom which they so highly treasure. However, the more they talk, the more it becomes apparent that they are also frightened by their "freedom." One realizes they are suffering from the feeling of social anomie which is a lack of purpose, identity, or ethical values in a person or society. It entails a certain amount of disorganization and rootlessness.

Rather than to view freedom as the ultimate achievement, it must also be recognized that a part of adult maturity is the capacity to tolerate commitment, intimacy, and responsibility. I have often been impressed that my own role as a counselor has changed considerably during the past ten years. During the early sixties, a major part of my counseling role was committed to helping people work through their hang-ups and to not be burdened by archaic guilt feelings which only hampered them in their efforts to gain a modicum of satisfaction from life. Since man's conscience is so malleable, many people have become victims of and advocates of the philosophical revolutions which I am discussing. As a result, my colleagues and I are seeing fewer people with hang-ups. We often comment that our role seems to have changed from one of helping people to become released from their "hang-ups" to that of trying to give people "hang-ups."

The notion of *giving* hang-ups suggests our belief that they will realize more satisfaction from life as they become able to tolerate commitment, intimacy, and responsibility. Also, I am frankly concerned that our society cannot survive if people do not become more "hung-up"—if hang-up is to mean the capacity to work, care for one's family, and to be concerned about the welfare of others.

The malleability of conscience has been alluded to. It is important to recognize that people can come to believe that almost anything is right. To this point, Dr. and Mrs. J. Wilke quote Edwin A. Roberts:

> Acts of great evil come easily to human nature. All that man's malleable conscience demands is a heroically articulated excuse combined with the comradeship of other evil-doers. In other

words, if the end is seen as both important and virtuous, then any means will often do. And the burden of solitary guilt need not be born if great numbers are also practicing the obscenity.

It is easier for a man to kill if those around him are killing, and it is easier for a man to kill if he has killed before. All fanatical tyrants have known this, from ancient oriental chieftains to Torquemada to Hitler to Mao. The moral instincts of humans are generally fragile, and if they are not constantly renewed by vigorous use, they wear away until they crumble completely.[7]

It is the capacity of people to believe anything is all right that demands that some of us oppose the popular notion that each person must make his personal decision and do what he thinks right. So that people will be prompted to examine the erroneous thinking basic to some of the revolutions, resistance to the popular philosophical revolutions must be offered.

The Myth Of Self-Fulfillment

The second characteristic common to the philosophical revolution is the concept of fulfillment. Unfortunately, fulfillment never seems to be adequately defined. Various catch phrases are used such as "doing one's thing," "not being victimized by traditional roles," "turns me on," etc. Also, the implication is that anything traditional is *ipso facto* unfulfilling.

Open Marriage by Neana and George O'Neill referred to in Section I is committed to helping its readers find self-fulfillment and freedom. Its phrases are selectively couched in verbiage that conveys the notion that if you oppose their concept of an open marriage, you're opposed to

---

[7]Dr. and Mrs. J. C. Wilke, *Handbook on Abortion,* Cincinnati, Ohio: Hiltz Publishing Co., 1971. (Quoted from Edwin A. Roberts, *National Observer,* January 18, 1972. Additional publication data not provided.), p. 115.

happiness and fulfillment. They cite the numerous examples of individuals who live together in trial marriages and decide to marry. Once they make a decision to enter into a marital contract, they discover that their relationship rapidly deteriorates. Consequently, within a year, they seek legal divorce and dissolve their once meaningful relationship. The authors believe this process of disaffection and alienation is precipitated by the entrance of the individuals into a marital contract in which they fall into stereotyped roles and become disillusioned by the marriage.

The O'Neills seemingly fail to recognize that perhaps these couples who succeed in trial marriage and fail in the committed marriage are unable to tolerate true commitment and that they may be frightened by the intimacy involved in a truly committed relationship. For many people, the inability to live in a committed relationship is caused by unresolved conflicts with their parents and parental figures. The entrance into traditional marriage rearouses their unresolved conflicts. For instance, I have known many spouses who have explained they were divorcing because they felt unfulfilled and that they felt unfulfilled because the marital relationship was sexually unrewarding. A spouse may explain that he or she will separate, become involved heterosexually with others, and seek to prove his or her sexual adequacy. Further discussion reveals that the person may have been involved in several extramarital affairs during which time sexual adequacy was no problem. It also develops that during the course of an extramarital affair, the spouses have been sexually competent not only with the paramour but also with the spouse. Also, once the firm decision is made do not become more "hung-up"—if hang-up is to mean the to separate, sexual adequacy with the spouse is recaptured. In many of these situations, ongoing therapy has demonstrated that the underlying problem was the inability to tolerate a committed relationship and that this inability was caused by the unresolved anger toward parents and parental figures. The marital relationship was symbolic of the proscriptions for living against which the distressed person needs to rebel.

It must also be recognized that there are various definitions of intimacy and various estimates as to the number of people who can tolerate an intimate relationship. The advocates of transactional analysis explain that about eighty percent of the population cannot actually tolerate intimacy. Perhaps this is an idea to which the advocates of open marriage should give some thought. Whereas they look at the individual who is favorable to the idea of an open marriage as being the mentally healthy and mature person, it is possible that these individuals are actually less fully developed, less fulfilled, and less mature than the person who can tolerate commitment and intimacy. The advocates of new life styles suggest that commitment and monogamy are necessary for insecure and jealous people. Perhaps what they look at as debilitating psychological hang-ups might be maturational achievements.

The fact that many people have problems with intimacy is obvious. It is recognized that "marriage makes strong demands for commitment to an adult identity which includes an ability to achieve ego differentiation and autonomy and to share emotional and sexual intimacy."[8] Although the challenge has been inadequately faced in traditional marriage, open marriage only circumvents the conundrum. The problem we have with intimacy has been discussed in various ways throughout this book. It is obvious that modern spouses must be challenged to come to grips with this fundamental difficulty in a way which enhances individual self-esteem, rein-

---

[8]Ruth C. Bullock, Rise Siegal, Myrna Weissman, and E. S. Paykel, "The Weeping Wife: Marital Relations of Depressed Women," *Journal of Marriage and The Family,* Vol. 34., No. 3, August, 1972, p. 492.

forces the sanctity of the marital bond, and preserves the dignity of marriage as a social institution.

As the advocates of open marriage make their case for extramarital friendships, their words and phrases are couched in such a way as to suggest that people ought to strive to be healthy enough to tolerate extramarital relationships both for themselves and for their spouse. Besides disagreeing with their basic premise that tolerance of extramarital relationships is indicative of health, I believe it must also be recognized that this philosophy has very serious ramifications for our society. There are several anthropological studies which suggest that promiscuous societies (and this is what would result from open marriages) do not survive. Studies by social anthropologists, J. P. Unwin and Pitirim Soikin[9] conclude that "civilization and culture depend upon the regulation of sexual expression and the confinement of sexual intercourse to monogamous homes and that where people are sexually 'free' and permissive, their culture deteriorates."

The fulfillment myth is evidenced in popular literature, advertising, and songs. The song, "I Got To Be Me," epitomizes this idea. The advocates of fulfillment fail to come to grips with a meaningful definition of fulfillment or to properly place this philosophy into a perspective which allows for the survival of society. The underlying assumption is that society exists for the good of the individual. They fail to consider that the ultimate conclusion of this concept is that society cannot survive when it is expected to satiate the selfish interests of each individual.

I have referred to fulfillment as a myth because I have serious doubt that fulfillment in the sense of using all of one's abilities to the maximum, being freed of the chore of

---

[9]Vernard Eller, *The Sex Manual for Puritans,* Nashville and New York: Abingdon Press, 1971, p. 43 (original reference not given).

nitty-gritty tasks, and being reasonably satisfied with self, others, and society is quite an impossible state of life to achieve. Also, I disagree with the philosophical revolutionaries because I do not believe fulfillment can be achieved unless one develops an underlying concern for the common good and unless one is concerned about the effect his actions will have upon the life of others. Also, I believe the false quest for fulfillment opens the door to highly competitive rather than corroborative relationships. I have frequently been impressed that people with massive doses of Not—OKness are flitting about under the guise of seeking fulfillment. They then seek to run over everyone else in an effort to gain an OK feeling. They fail to recognize that a sense of OKness emanates from an internalized feeling of worth rather than from showing that one is more fulfilled than anyone else.

One should seek to be fulfilled, in the sense that fulfillment is an effort to utilize one's capacities to the maximum. On the other hand, it must be recognized that complete temporal fulfillment is impossible. In seeking fulfillment, one must place into perspective the needs of others and the needs of the general society. This other directedness may temporarily frustrate one in his efforts to gain fulfillment. At any rate, this temporary frustration is relatively inconsequential compared to the chaos the larger society will experience if its members are selfishly locked in on their own fulfillment needs. This leads us to the next philosophical revolution which is concerned with the common good.

Individual Fulfillment
vs.
The Common Good

Many of us were exposed to the ethic that one could not perform or commit an act without assessing the effect the performance or commission of that act would have upon others. It is undeniable that this emphasis upon the rights of others had an adverse effect upon the rights of many individuals. However, we seem now to be at a point where the situation is reversed. Now, it seems that the individual thinks only of the effect a particular piece of behavior is going to have upon himself. Because of the emphasis upon individual rights, the rights of others and especially the rights of institutions such as marriage and government are given little consideration.

Society will pay a high price if its members continue to accept an ideology which encourages people to do whatever seems to turn them on. Instead, we must more strongly emphasize the effect an individual's behavior will have upon the common good. It must be stressed that individuals cannot act in favor of their own benefit without having thoroughly assessed the ramification and effect that behavior will have upon the common good. Many have expressed concern that this ideology may cooperate in creating a group of self-centered and narcissistic individuals who have no tolerance for the opinions of others and who are quite unable to participate in a system of communication or government based upon consensus. Society is now at a point where it must find the middle ground between the one extreme of emphasizing the common good at the expense of the individual good and the other extreme of emphasizing the individual's rights over and above the common good.

Related to the concern about the common good is the concern that we come to grips with what is realistic and what is neurotic guilt. In counseling, I am frequently faced with a situation in which one spouse expresses the wish to become involved in an affair with another person. The husband or wife may feel that the affair would be personally helpful and in the end, believes that it would be helpful to the marriage. The spouse frequently explains that the involvement in an affair will increase the capacity to cope with the other spouse. In many instances, the person expecting to become involved in an affair realizes that he or she is considering involvement in a very risky situation. There are several situations in which the other spouse may seem to function quite competently. However, there may be a paranoid base to the personality which causes the spouse to accuse the other of being involved in affairs even when the other is not so involved. In discussing these situations, the spouse considering the affair frequently realizes that if the other spouse becomes aware of this involvement, homicide and/or suicide remain as real possibilities.

In discussing this with me, the spouse considering the affair may explain that he or she has some guilt feelings and some fears about the affair and yet does not want to abandon the idea. I frequently explain that I believe that guilt about this intention is normal and healthy. In talking about the normality of the guilt, I have explained that the fears were realistic. Spouses have often stated that they wish I would tap them on the shoulder, say that everything was OK, that there was nothing to feel guilty about, and that everything would turn out all right. But I have the Judeo-Christian hang-up about extramarital affairs and I believe that guilt is a very appropriate reaction. In addition, I have explained that to allay the fears about the reaction of the other spouse would be unrealistic and misleading.

In essence, it is more helpful to people to explain the normality of guilt than to allay what is really a healthy psychological and moral reaction. Also, this reaction on the part of a therapist or counselor has a more positive ramification for our society in general. It is not advantageous to have people who have no capacity for guilt and who are able to rationalize all of their behavior so as to come to a feeling of self-righteousness. It seems that this is a situation in which the welfare both of the individual and of the larger society is better served by recognizing the normality of certain guilt and fear reactions.

It must also be recognized that many are "turned off" by any discussion of guilt. This super-reaction is frequently understood once it is realized that the person who experiences a strong repugnance to any discussion of guilt was, in his developmental years, exposed to a hell and damnation type of religion. Many of them were Guilty Miltys or Millys who resolved the problem of their neurotic guilt by kicking over all the traces of the past. Any attempt at rational discussion of normal guilt reminds them of the distortions of their earlier teaching. They think of all guilt as horrible, and fail to understand what is normal guilt.

The second-rate status given to the common good was demonstrated in an article entitled the "Dropout Wife." The author explains that one evening, thirty-five year old Wanda Lee Adams, college graduate, wife of a middle-level Seattle executive and mother of three, walked out on her family to begin a new life on her own. She had begun to see her life as increasingly frustrating and suffocating. Shortly after marriage, she was teaching kindergarten in order to supplement her husband's rather meager income. After some fourteen years of marriage, she started to work again and enjoyed it. She went back to school and there encountered the Woman's Liberation Movement. "I then realized," she said, "that I was experiencing what a lot of women experience. Don was a decent human being who had allowed me to grow to a certain point. But, past that point, I had to leave." And she did. The breakup of a home for such cool reasons is no longer rare. Most dropouts are middle-class, educated, highly motivated women who have been married a number of years.

Mrs. Adams explained that in her new life she was far happier than she ever had been. In spite of the loneliness, struggle for survival, and the occasional feelings of not wanting to be independent, she reported that she liked herself better and liked other people better. At the time the article was written, she had a ten year old daughter living with her and the husband had custody of the two sons, one of whom had a severe hearing loss.

She conceived of herself as an object lesson. She explained that she didn't think marriage was a rewarding, fulfilling life. It was merely adequate. She explained that married women were kidding themselves if they didn't realize they were going to need more than just a marriage in life.

It appears that Mrs. Adams is representative of the people who are finding happiness at the expense of others. There is no concern expressed for the father, for the two boys who are left behind not being able to understand what their mother is doing, and for whether or not this free life is really good for the ten year old daughter who is living with her. The rights of the individual are being expressed at the expense of the lives of the other members of the family. One must seriously consider whether there should be admonishment for this kind of behavior or if it should be looked upon as being very cool and sophisticated.[10]

In contrast to Mrs. Adams, Ben Ard has wondered whether middle-class values are all bad. He believes:

> Some of the much maligned middle-class values may be necessary for a technologically advanced society such as ours to survive, e.g., punctuality, a certain minimum of reliability and accountability (if not responsibility), as well as a minimum of orderliness (which is not the same as a compulsive form of orderliness). . . .
>
> A certain amount of postponement of instant satisfaction in the "here and now" may be necessary to learn practically any discipline, if we are to continue to have doctors, engineers, scientists, etc. This does not mean that a puritanical rejection of all "pleasure" is desirable. The learning of a minimum of skills (reading,

---

[10]"Dropout Wife," *Life*, March 17, 1972, Vol. 72, No. 10, pp. 34B-45.

writing, etc.) is necessary for a literate if not enlightened and electorate. All the values that "schools" stand for are not necessarily completely bad. . . .

Neither do all people have to live in the traditional forms of marriage and the family, or become parents. Sex is a positive value for human beings who are healthy psychologically, although middle-class values have traditionally been anti-sex and our culture indiscriminate, instant intimacy is not the only alternative to middle-class conventionalities regarding sex, however.[11]

People frequently become involved in conversations in which they begin to talk about what this person or that person has done. One of the magic responses while discussing the behavior is to say, "I may not agree with what he has done, but I certainly support his right to make his own decision." Emphasis is placed upon the notion that the individual has made a decision and that is interpreted as a wonderful phenomenon. However, it is necessary to question whether or not the decision was correct, and to judge the effect that decision is having upon the common good. It is recognized that whether or not a decision is good or bad is a subjective evaluation. However, because of our intoxication with the idea of self-fulfillment and our emphasis upon individual rights, we sometimes deny people the benefit of our subjective opinions which may be at variance with their own. These opinions may provide them with the opportunity to make a more reasonable decision.

I Am Sorry, I Have Found Someone Else

This is a philosophy which is very much a part of the revolutionary thinking which is undermining the fundamental

---

[11]Ben N. Ard, "Are All Middle-Class Values Bad?" *The Family Coordinator*, April, 1972, p. 223.

nature of marriage as a relationship and as an institution. We have heard much discussion about group marriages and the general idea of reaching a point in the marriage where one simply tires of the other, decides that it would be well to go one's own way and to take up with a new-found "true love." Several couples have placed me in a predicament as one spouse asks for marriage counseling and the other, in essence, requests divorce counseling. The one asking for divorce counseling is saying, "I am sorry, but I have no love for you, I have found someone with whom I can share a very deep love, and I wish you would let me go before we hurt each other any more." The other spouse asks, "Well, if there is something wrong with our marriage, should we seek to straighten it out rather than to simply go ahead with divorce?" To this, the other replies, "Why should I work so hard to straighten out a marriage when I am already involved with somebody who turns me on and someone with whom I can find 'true happiness'." The spouse asking for the divorce feels no responsibility toward making an effort to make the present marriage work. He or she is saying, "I want to be 'free', I want to lead the 'free life', and I do not want to be tied down."

A decade ago, society and counselors looked upon this as evidence of at least a minimal degree of psychopathology. What frightens me at this time is that in most instances, a therapist cannot make a case for the presence of psychopathology. If there was evidence of psychopathology, one might then be able to treat the sickness or at least the reaction would be recognized as abnormal. It seems that people making these statements are victims of and/or participants in a philosophical revolution. They are participating in a philosophical notion which essentially says that all happiness is to be found here on earth, there is no hereafter, (or else they may say that God intended for us to be happy on earth), and we should not be all bogged down by responsibility. If one is not happy with his plight, he should get out of it rather than to make an effort to improve the conditions of the present situation.

In this type of situation, the counselor must gain some idea of the thinking of each spouse. He can frequently come to understand how each spouse perceives his role by explaining that there are three mental attitudes that spouses bring to the counseling situation: (1) The super-positive attitude is exemplified by the couple that says, "We have a great investment in this relationship and we must find a way to make it more rewarding." (2) The opposite mental attitude is depicted by the couple who explains, "We are doing a great deal of damage to each other. The most helpful and constructive course of action for us to take is to let each other go. Please help us to find the best possible way to break away from each other." (3) The moderate mental attitude is manifested by the couple who explain, "We really do not know what we are doing to each other, we do not understand our relationship, we do not know what the future holds for us, but we do want to explore all of these unknowns in order to see whether or not it is wise and healthy for us to continue our marriage." If each spouse maintains the same mental attitude, the counselor's role is not nearly so ambiguous as when one spouse is at position one and the other is at position two.

I have seen many situations in which one spouse is at position one and the other at position two. The spouse in position one is frequently left with children to care for, inadequate financial support, and many unrealized hopes and dreams. Above and beyond all, the spouse who is left behind wonders, "What happened? What changed so much? What do I do now?" There is often no sickness on the part of the spouse who is leaving the marriage, but they have changed their life style and value system. After seeing many spouses who have been left behind, I have been overwhelmingly impressed with the inherent inequality of life. As no family *deserves* to be struck by the premature death of a spouse, these families do not *deserve* to be struck by divorce.

The spouse who is left behind seems to have two alternatives. The first is to assume the Monica syndrome. Monica, the mother of St. Augustine, patiently prayed for years that her wayward son would be open to the grace of the spirit and return to the fold. After several years, her prayers were answered. After about five years' experience with the philosophical revolutions, I am beginning to see some of the benefits of the Monica reaction. Spouses who have left their marriages are beginning to see that the free life is not fulfilling and some are returning to their families.

The second reaction is to work through one's guilt, anger, and remorse about what happened in the marriage, and to then seek to make a new life for oneself. A new life may mean training for and the pursuit of a career and/or it may mean remarriage. The prospect of remarriage assumes many difficult dimensions for people of the religious faiths which do not recognize divorce and remarriage. These divorcees are often placed in the difficult position of needing to choose between remarriage and being able to continue as active participants in their church.[12]

In the situation described above, one sees one of the more painful things that can happen to spouses. They marry at a time when they agree upon values, norms, and goals. One

---

[12]The plight of some divorcees is being somewhat lightened for members of the Catholic Church wherein which many diocesan tribunals are interpreting the validity of marriage on a broader scale. For instance, it was generally common to nullify marriages on the grounds of mental incapacity only in situations in which psychosis was evident. In recent years, some tribunals are beginning to recognize that spouses who are psychologically incapable of entering into a committed and intimate union are also incapable of entering into a valid marriage. It should not be thought that the commitment to exclusive and monogamous marriage is in any way being compromised. The tribunals are simply utilizing the evolving insights and knowledge of the behavioral sciences in an effort to more totally evaluate the validity of various marriages.

partner or the other may become involved in life in such a way that his values, norms, and standards undergo change. One spouse may completely modify his life style. For instance, several people begin marriage with a "home and hearth" concept of marriage. During the course of the marriage, they are exposed to different life experiences and to different people. As a result of these different life experiences, one or the other may become estranged from the "home and hearth" as a value and become more taken up with a style of life which allows them to "be free." The unfortunate victim of this change may remain oriented to "home and hearth" and just stand back wondering whatever has happened to the dreams and aspirations which they shared.

Perhaps this is best exemplified in Lillian Helman's play, *Toys In The Attic,* in which she talks about people who are faced with the truth of another person. She makes the painful observation which expresses the situation for many couples: "Well, people change and they forget to tell each other. Too bad—causes so many mistakes."

Again, it must be reiterated that a change between the seventies and the fifties is that many people now feel free to divorce. The philosophical revolutions have made divorce at least acceptable and, in some circles, it provides people with an esteemed status. Some people look upon divorce as indicative of one's coolness, modness, and sophistication. Divorce becomes a sign that one is not hung-up and that he will not be constrained by any "outmoded" responsibilities which hinder him in his quest for fulfillment. It is no longer "in" to stay together for the sake of the children.

Research has indicated that children seem to be more adversely affected by living with parents who should be getting a divorce than they are by actually becoming the products of the divorce. Many marriage and family counselors now find themselves in a peculiar predicament. A generation ago, we might have explained to people that their children would perhaps be better off if they divorced rather than to continue the life together in which they assaulted each other's dignity with a refined violence. Now, in the seventies, spouses come to us explaining that the children would actually be better off if they divorced and anyway, "I'm not going to ruin my life for the next five-ten years just for the kids." We now have to ask some of these people whether or not their marriage could succeed if they were willing to work at it and if, in that instance, the children's welfare might be better served.

Although a child's overall adjustment may not be adversely affected by divorce, there is a happiness factor which cannot be measured. Many children are saddened by divorce and it seems feasible that they would have been happier if their parents had been willing to work at the marriage. Essentially, I am asking that we question the wisdom of authorities [13] who view divorce as a desirable social necessity and not a personal calamity. There are many personal, interpersonal, and social calamities surrounding divorce. I disagree that greater freedom to abort and premarital sex form a new base for giving new worth to the human being.

I certainly recognize that in some situations divorce is a very feasible alternative. At this juncture, I am expressing my objection to divorces which arise out of a need on the part of one party or the other to prove his coolness and because of a refusal to work at a relationship. It does have to be recognized that there are some marriages which cannot work out. For these people, they are doing both themselves and their children a favor by separating or divorcing.

---

[13]Virginia Satir, *op. cit*, p. 303.

Let's Make Sure It Can Work

One of the phenomena which must be recognized as common to all of the philosophical revolutions is that they are more talked about and intellectually accepted than actually practiced. The large majority of the population does not leave its spouse and children for a new mate, does not disregard the rights of others, and does not think marriage is an outdated and archaic institution. There are some people who totally reject the dictates of the philosophical revolution, others who accept them as "all right for those who like it, but it's not for me," and a small percentage of the population who become active participants in the philosophical revolutions. When we talk about the popularity of any of these revolutions, it must be remembered that the idea is more popular than the overt implementation of the idea. As this is true for the revolutions so far discussed, it is also true for trial marriages and the various spin-offs of that idea. Trial marriages are designed to enable people to live together for awhile, experiment with their compatibility, and to only enter into marriage after they have become certain that they can find fulfillment in a committed relationship to each other. In some of Robert Rimmer's books such as *The Harrad Experiment* and *Proposition 31,* he has popularized the concept of trial marriage and the idea of heterosexual and noncommitted living together as a vehicle for the achievement of personal growth. Some attention has also been given to the concept in professional literature. The results of the various studies are ambiguous and there is a paucity of *objective* research. As one reviews the professional literature, one is left with the impression that if the researcher favors the idea of trial or multilateral marriages, the results of his study suggest that these are viable alternatives to traditional marriage. On the other hand, if the researcher seems personally opposed to these alternative styles, his research suggests that these alternatives have a harmful effect upon the individuals involved. Apparently, the general area of alternatives to marriage has not yet merited the interest of solid academic research.

It must be recognized that the term trial marriage is a misnomer. One can never really give a try at marriage as one has to actually be involved in a committed relationship before one really has a chance of making it work. Also, once the commitment is made to marriage, people do modify their behavior in that they may make less of an effort to be pleasing and satisfying to their partner.

Also, many people enter into trial marriages because of the many unhappy marriages they have seen. They hope that a trial marriage will be the best way to select their mate and to insure against future marital discord. Many young married couples become totally disillusioned when they experience conflict in marriage. Because of the sensitivity to conflict, they assume that the overt manifestation of this discord indicates that they are not meant for each other and that their marriage is doomed. For this reason, many young couples, who have been exposed to the philosophical revolution, will first seek the services of an attorney rather than to contact a counselor who might help them discover ways in which they can effectively adapt to each other.

As I have suggested earlier, I am frequently impressed by the number of people who try to be very cool and mod in their attitudes toward interpersonal relationships, but who, in the final analysis, have a difficult time pulling it all off. I am reminded of the girl who came to a marriage counselor. She was shattered over the break-up of her eighteen-month affair with a young man. During the course of her interview, the counselor asked her what it was she thought he might help her do. She wanted him to help her restore the broken relationship, help her to get the fellow back from the other woman. The marriage counselor asked her what sort of a relationship it was they had she wished to restore. She replied that it was, "like we were married, but not married." He asked why they had chosen to live like they were married, but not get married. She responded, "Because we both wanted to be free." "Free to do what?" "Free to break it off. Free of real commitment. . . ."

It is with these philosophical revolutions in mind that spouses must consider the quality and style of marriage they desire.

Styles For Marriage

Modern spouses are faced with placing into perspective the pressures the general society places upon marriage and seeking to determine a type and style of marriage they desire. The type and quality of marriage is not a matter left to the fates. In an effort to enhance the quality of their marriage, couples are free to implement the suggestions made in this book as well as the help available to them in other books and through other resources such as retreats and workshops. It is certainly recognized that experts cannot tell people how they are supposed to live their married life. In one sense, people are prone to reject didactic advice that is given to them. People often exclaim, "I want some black and white answers!" I frequently comment, "I would be happy to provide the black and white answers, but I fear that would only provide you with another reason for not doing what is necessary to effect a rewarding marriage." This statement applies to the people who may operate from an I'm Not-OK; You're Not-OK position. They need to prove that there are no answers for their problems and that their relationship can never work out. They need to validate their own inadequacy as well as that of the experts. This, of course, speaks to the extreme situation. In the more universal sense, black and white answers are not feasible because people have to assess the didactic advice which is given and, depending upon their own interests and personality traits, selectively utilize the insights provided by behavioral scientists, clergy, and poets. For instance, it is wonderful if people do not shout at each other. However, one does have to take into consideration the temperaments that are involved and to consider the way in which shouting may lead to a constructive end.

The advice of experts is frequently ineffective because spouses will often utilize it in a scatter-gun way. For instance, they may read an article and decide they will try to conduct their marriage in the way advised. After a couple of weeks, they find that approach is not working, turn to another author, and follow his advice. Couples must be much more eclectic in their approach to marriage. The advice couples use for their marriage is perhaps much like their household furniture—early eclectic. That is, they should assess what they read, determine the way in which the advice could be utilized, and then selectively apply it in the light of their own interests and temperament.

It is the wise couple who approaches their marriage in an artistic fashion. The artist, in contrast to the technician, has some general guidelines and principles which are applied as the situation demands. The artist has very few definite laws which will apply to each and every situation. He cannot readily turn to a manual which describes the steps to follow in solving a particular problem. He must selectively follow guidelines and principles.

Couples are in a position to decide upon the style and quality of marriage they want. Although there are several ways in which one can describe styles for and the quality of marriage, four particular styles will now be considered. These are the "zilchy" or the minimal expectation relationship, the senescent marriage, the ultimate satisfaction marriage, and the warm and rewarding relationship.

The Minimal Expectation Marriage

One of the unfortunate ramifications of this choice is that if one of the spouses objects to this style and strives for a higher quality relationship, he will find himself stagnated at the level of the other spouse who has a minimal expectation for the relationship. This relates to the concept discussed in Section III in which it was suggested that the amount of satisfaction that can be realized from a relationship is equal to the minimal amount of effort exerted by the spouse least interested in the marriage.

In this zilchy marriage, we find the husband and/or the wife effectively play or plays the role of a "slob." In the instance of the male, this may be a genuine chauvinist who feels that a woman's role is to serve man. She is to care for all of his physical needs (including sexual as that is not considered an emotional need for this individual), take care of the house, take care of whatever children happen to come along, and in general be available where and when he wants her. He (and this may very well be she) seems to have little capacity for emotional warmth and tenderness. This is the individual who feels that he is his own man, no one is going to tell him what to do, and he is beholden to no one. He believes that as long as he supports his family and as long as no one is hungry or without clothes, he is doing his job. He goes to work, stops for a few beers or drinks after work, comes home and wants supper ready for him, watches a bit of TV, goes to bed, and may or may not sneeze in the loins of his wife (this cannot be referred to as intercourse, but it is really more of a masturbatory experience where the partner is a passive object for masturbation), wakes up the next morning and may or may not again have intercourse, have his breakfast, and head off for work. The routine is modified on Friday night when he has a few more drinks after work and gets home somewhat later than the other nights of the week. He then settles down on Saturday and Sunday for a stimulating weekend of TV which enables him to vicariously resolve his psychic conflicts by enjoying the feats of one athletic hero after the other.

The pattern for the woman who opts for the minimal expectation marriage is much like that of the husband. She exerts little or no effort to improve the quality of the marriage and to make home life a pleasant and rewarding experience.

Many of the persons who opt for this type of relationship labor under the burden of a marked degree of Not-OKness. Because of their inadequacy, they feel they have nothing to offer. As suggested in Chapter 8, everyone needs to feel significant. In many instances, one gains significance from being undesirable. For instance, one's significance may arise from the capacity to outdrink anyone in the bar, from having the most traffic tickets of anyone in the plant, or from being the sloppiest housekeeper of any of the relatives.

The Senescent Marriage

This relationship was described in the first chapter where it was suggested that carelessness about the relationship is one of the most serious problems experienced in marriage. This style is representative of the greater share of the population who fail to recognize the importance of working at marriage. They are like the couple who were sitting in their kitchen enjoying a cup of coffee when they heard a terrific explosion coming from the house next to them. Rushing to the window, they saw their neighbors come flying out the window from the force of the explosion, and the man turned to his wife and said, "That's the first time those two have been out together since they were married." If it is always too much trouble to get ready, or one or the other is always too tired, the couples get out of the habit of going out together. But, "getting out of the habit" leads to a new habit which is deadly. Lee and Casebier explain that when there is simply the same routine each evening, the same television programs, if there are no outside contacts to bring new interest and pleasure into the life of the marriage, the stage is set for the vague restlessness, emptiness, dullness, sameness that spells "boredom." They refer to the "four B's syndrome": Bridge, Bourbon, Bon-bons, and Boredom.[14] They go on to explain that the most serious B is that of Boredom as it gnaws at one's soul. They quote Balzac saying that " 'Marriage must constantly conquer the monster that devours. The name of that monster is habit.' Habits, patterns, routines, when they remain unexamined, lead finally to monumental boredom and ennui. The stable, dependable, orderly routine which once implied security in the marital relationship now becomes a dreaded marriage rut. Spouses cease to apply spice in the marriage relationship and the gap becomes an ugly ditch that divides and separates husband and wife."[15]

The Ultimate Fulfillment Marriage

Many of the spouses opting for this style of marriage have been exposed to the thinking of the "sensitivity buffs" who believe in indepth communication and who maintain that the maximum and ultimate in fulfillment must be experienced. The difficulty is that people disagree on the definition of indepth communication. It is found that indepth communication to one person is intellectualization to another, indepth to someone else is small talk to another, indepth to another is

---

[14]Robert Lee and Marjorie Casebier, *The Spouse Gap*, Nashville and New York: Abingdon Press, 1971, p. 87.

[15]*Ibid.*, pp. 14-15.

rationalization to a spouse, etc. These are often the people who have become part of the philosophical revolutions. They seem to be reading one book after the other, attending seminars, and participating in sensitivity sessions in the hope of finding the experience that will provide the ultimate turn-on and give them the fulfillment for which they are searching. Their expectations are laudable, but it seems they expect the marital relationship to deliver more than is feasible for a human relationship which focuses exclusively upon temporal rewards. One gets the feeling they are hoping that interpersonal relationships will compensate for internal feelings of inadequacy. Unfortunately, they have ill-defined the problem, have looked for a solution that is not feasible, the problem goes unresolved, and the frustration avalanches. It seems that the communication is never deep enough, the relationship is never meaningful enough, and the amount and degree of sharing is always inadequate.

The advocates of this style believe that part of the ultimate potential for marriage lies in: (1) the evolving freedom women are experiencing professionally and economically, (2) their freedom from household drudgery, and (3) the fact that women are becoming sexually liberated. It must readily be granted that these three freedoms enable spouses to find a new meaning to their relationship. However, the freedoms must be dealt with responsibly and realistically.

Unfortunately, the advocates of this style have little time for the "have to" things of life that are not particularly challenging or stimulating. They believe that people are expressing only ten percent of their creativity. They maintain that being "freed up" and involved in an open relationship will enable one to realize a greater percent of his potential.

Marriage is not viewed as an economic necessity, but a relationship in which people come to be emotionally dependent upon each other. They are looking for marriage to bring the ultimate in: (1) communication, (2) intimacy, (3) sexual satisfaction, and (4) ecstasy.

As much as there is a great risk to be experienced by those who do not take their marriage seriously, a risk is also experienced by those who are obsessed with the idea of continually improving the quality of communication, the sexual relationship, and the growth potential to be provided by the marriage. It is soon realized that one can die from anxiety about growth as well as from atrophy.

The Warm and Rewarding Marriage

The spouses who strive for this style of marriage are able to accept the challenge of marriage and to view it as a meaningful job and task. They look at their love in a dynamic way and view their relationship in an artistic fashion. This type of marriage was alluded to in Section I where I referred to Karl and to the man meeting his wife at the airport. They place the idea of dependence and independence into a proper perspective and thereby attain a rewarding feeling of interdependence. As much as they are able to be interdependent in their relationship with each other, they are also able to realize an interdependence with God. They realize that all human relationships are limited by the simple fact of humanness. They appreciate their interpersonal differences. This appreciation of differences provides a built-in growth potential. They seek to adapt to and accommodate themselves to each other. They realize that needing each other is not indicative of a neurotic sense of dependence. Rather than to compete and to prove themselves more equal than the other, they strive to develop a corroborative relationship.

CHAPTER 19

The Spiritual Dimension

After reviewing the nature of marriage, personality, inter-personal communication, sexuality, philosophical revolutions, and styles of marriage, we are ultimately left with the question about the future of marriage. It is granted that venerated ideas of yesteryear like "the bonds of marriage," "the institution of marriage," or the "vocation of marriage" no longer impress a number of people. Nor do many people stand at attention when someone speaks of the "sacramentality of marriage" or marriage as a "life-long commitment"—notions they can hardly understand, given the "Why marry?" attitude. Where love is freely given, why speak of vows? Given the freedom of choice to love each other, why speak of contract?

The Now Generation does not easily see the consequences that result from marriage becoming a purely consensual affair between two individuals. They are not aware that their "love freely given" is most likely neither free nor love. Many do not appreciate the radically social character of human nature and indeed of marriage itself. True, the decision to marry or to engage in a marriage relationship is a most personal one, but it inherently involves many others. Because of the social consequences stemming from this most personal decision and thus involving the community and inherently a public commitment along with a private promise or vow, all of the experience and anthropological data point to the need of some kind of public witness before two people live together "in love" as committed partners.[1] Recognizing the existence of this thinking, the person committed to traditional marriage is comforted by Leo XIII's advice that, "We must see the world as it really exists and often look elsewhere for the solace of its troubles."

Many of the revolters and the disenchanted explain that the traditional Judeo-Christian approach to marriage has not worked. Therefore, they reason, alternative styles must be tried to see if they can be more rewarding to spouses. What is forgotten is that the Judeo-Christian approach to marriage fails when it is not really tried. Inherent within the Judeo-Christian approach is commitment to God and a realization that the marital relationship is designed to be a part of His perfection. Implied within this tradition is the demand that couples develop a deep and meaningful spiritual life in which they recognize their earthly existence as transitory and in which they realize they are striving for another Kingdom. When the Judeo-Christian approach is accepted in entirety, it can offer a degree of happiness never to be approached by the alternative styles. The difficulty is that spouses resist taking the leap in which they truly turn things over to God. However, it must be reiterated that the traditional approach cannot be criticized because most people do not really give it a full try. It cannot be criticized unless we are like Zacchaeus who had climbed a tree to gain a glimpse of the Lord. The Lord saw him and said He was coming to his house. When Zacchaeus let the Lord into his house, his whole life was changed. (Luke 19) When the Lord is taken into marriage, the quality of the relationship assumes a transcendental dimension which offers true fulfillment.

---

[1]The above two paragraphs, by the author and Paul Marx, were previously published in "Family Life: The Agony and the Ecstasy," *Future of the Family,* (Ed. Clayton C. Barbeau) New York: Bruce Publishing Company, 1971.

Will marriage survive? Undoubtedly. From the beginning of mankind, no substitute has ever been discovered. What shape it will take is impossible to describe at this time. How Judeo-Christian marriage will fare in an increasingly material-istic and Hedonistic world will depend on the extent to which spouses follow the late Cardinal Suhard's advice: "We should live in this world in such a way that our life would not make sense if God did not exist." The dynamic, adaptive couple will survive until Gabriel blows his trumpets calling all of us to join in the eternal joys of the Father's family in heaven. We are members of the People of God who, in a sense, are groping in a new Diaspora.